Beyond
THE LAUNCH

BEYOND
THE LAUNCH

*The Practical Guide to Building
a Business that Thrives*

Joellyn Sargent

BRAND
SPROUT®
BOOKS

Published by BrandSprout® Books, Milton, Georgia

This book is designed to provide accurate and authoritative information in regard to the subject matter covered. It is sold with the understanding that neither the author nor publisher is engaged in rendering legal, accounting or other professional services. If legal advice or other expert assistance is required, the services of a competent professional should be sought.

Quantity sales: special discounts are available on bulk purchases by corporations, associations, and other eligible groups. For details, call 678-823-8228.

Publisher's Cataloging-in-Publication Data:

Sargent, Joellyn 1966–

    Beyond the launch: the practical guide for building a business that thrives / Joellyn Sargent

        p. cm.

    Includes biographical references and index.

    ISBN 978-0615994888

    1. Entrepreneurship   2. Small Business   3. Marketing   I. Title

Library of Congress Control Number: 2014906302

Printed in the United States of America.

10 9 8 7 6 5 4 3 2 1

To John & Rebecca,
my endless source of inspiration.

Contents

Introduction

Where Do You Go From Here?

There are lots of books about starting a business. A quick search on Amazon turns up thousands of titles on the subject (as I write this, 17,814 and counting). Some of these books offer tips on finding the right idea and defining your concept. Others are step-by-step guides to get started when the entrepreneurial bug bites.

But what happens after the Grand Opening? The ribbon cutting ceremony is over. The bubbly is gone and the toasts are merely a memory. The cake crumbs have been swept up from the floor. Your baby, the idea you worked so hard to nurture, is now a *bona fide* business, ready to stand on its own.

Whether you've been running your company for ten months or ten years, you've discovered that finding the right advice when you need it is an ongoing challenge for business owners.

With new businesses opening at a record pace—the Kauffman Foundation reported that 514,000 Americans opened a new business *every month* in 2012[1]—the question is not how to start a business, but how to keep it growing.

---

[1]Fairlie, Robert W. 2013. *Kauffman Index of Entrepreneurial Activity*. 2. Ewing Marion Kauffman Foundation.

My personal experiences building several different companies taught me that starting a business is the easy part. Almost anyone can launch a new venture for a few hundred bucks. Making it thrive? That's another thing altogether.

Beyond the Launch is when the real work begins.

Like you, many of my consulting clients find themselves challenged by the increasing difficulties of cultivating a vibrant company. I help them navigate the choppy waters of building a business and sustaining growth so they can enjoy the fruits of their efforts.

In the pages that follow, I'll help you, too. Inside this book you'll discover a wealth of practical advice and actionable tips you can apply immediately to improve your business results.

When Fantasy Fades

It's not uncommon for the romance of *"Wouldn't it be great if..."* to fade away as your business matures. Dreams of unbridled success are quickly replaced by the reality of day-to-day routines and the challenges of meeting payroll, retaining great employees and making sure your best customers keep coming back.

What happens when your dreams start to look a little less rosy and the painful truth that running a business can be hard—really hard—starts to set in?

No matter how new or established your business, there are bound to be days when you wonder, *"Why did I think this was a good idea?"* There will be times when you think you never should have started and days when you consider throwing in the towel. **Don't.**

It's true, running a company can be difficult. The highs and lows that make being your own boss both fruitful and frustrating are simply part of the process. The right advice and expert guidance can make the experience of entrepreneurship much more rewarding, allowing you to focus on why you started your business in the first place.

This book is about what you need to know so you can get—and stay—on track. There is no magic formula for success. It takes hard work, persistence, and patience. If you have those three things (and I'm willing to bet you do, or you wouldn't have picked up this book) follow the words of advice contained in this volume and you'll be well on your way to a more successful business.

How to Use this Book

I know you're busy, so I have organized this book into topical sections that are easy to scan when you have just a few minutes to tackle a challenge. You can certainly start at the beginning and work your way through, building a better business one step at a time. If that's not your style, just dive right in to the section that looks most interesting.

No matter how you approach it, you'll discover this book is packed with valuable lessons and tips to make those frustrating days less frequent, helping you enjoy your business and live the dream that lead you here in the beginning.

Note: The examples in this book are drawn from my own experience and my work with clients running real businesses. In certain cases, I have fictionalized companies and their owners in respect for privacy. Other cases are amalgamations of common situations, representing recurring patterns that business owners face.

Chapter 1

Getting Started: Where Do You Stand?

No matter how successful your business is, I'll hazard a guess that it's not quite where you want it to be. Entrepreneurs tend to dream big, seeking more, better, faster, and constantly looking toward the horizon.

Like many readers, you probably picked up this book for one of two reasons:

1) There's a problem standing between you and the success you seek, *or*
2) There are opportunities out there you have not (yet) captured, and you need a little boost to get there.

Either way, there's an upside for you, so let's get right to work.

We'll begin by determining which, if not both, of these issues apply to you. First, we'll take a look at ways to evaluate the true nature of the problems you may be facing. Then we will explore opportunities lying just beneath the surface, waiting for you to seize them. In both cases, I'll offer actionable approaches to moving forward so you can build the business of your dreams.

Identify Your Issues

If your business isn't delivering the results you want, you might assume that you know the source of your trouble. "We need more customers," you think. Maybe you have the wrong location, unhappy employees, products that do not appeal to buyers, prices that are too high—or even too low. If you just had a new website, updated equipment or that new software release, everything would be great, right?

Not likely.

No matter how obvious the problem seems to be, the best way to solve it is not to jump right in with a solution that appears to be a no-brainer. Stop for a minute and think…do you *really* know the root of your problem? Odds are it is not as readily apparent as you think.

Often what looks like an isolated problem is, in reality, a symptom of a larger underlying issue with the business. When something is wrong, your ability to find and fix it can mean the difference between success and failure. If you do not treat the right problem, the one that is actually the source of the symptoms, business will continue to suffer until you discover the root cause.

Jumping to the wrong conclusion can be a fatal business error for new and seasoned entrepreneurs alike. In fact, if you've been in business for a while, you might fall into the trap more easily, assuming your experience means you have *"been there, done that."*

In spite of what you might think, you haven't seen it all.

Seeking the Source

Let's explore the example of an established remodeling company that is suddenly scrambling for new customers:

Tom is a former accountant who loves rolling up his sleeves and renovating homes. After flipping a few foreclosed homes, he decided to start his own business using his skills to help homeowners create the living spaces they dreamed about. Tom started HomeScape Remodeling three years ago and enjoyed immediate success.

Business was so good for the first couple of years that Tom hired two sales reps to meet with prospective clients. He expanded his construction team and got lots of referrals from clients for new projects in neighborhoods where he had previously worked.

Some time after his third anniversary, Tom's business slowed to a trickle. Referrals dribbled in and he got a few calls from his ads in the local paper, but he wasn't generating nearly as much business as he needed to make ends meet.

Tom assumed he had a marketing problem. He needed more new customers, so he pulled out all the stops, launching a radio campaign and sending postcard mailings to most of the addresses in town. His marketing costs went up and he won a few new customers, but the profitability of Tom's business continued to decline.

Tom couldn't keep up with the marketing expense required to bring in new business, so he sought outside help.

"I don't get it," said Tom. "I'm marketing like crazy, but I can't seem to get ahead of the game."

Let's look back and see what Tom might have missed:

1) He had solid referral business for a couple of years, but then the referrals suddenly slowed down.
2) Tom was bringing in new customers, but they didn't provide the quality or quantity of referrals he used to enjoy.
3) The timing of this decline was a few months after Tom hired his sales staff, delegating responsibility for a task he had previously performed himself.

It turns out Tom's problem was not a marketing issue, it was a sales and service problem.

In their zeal to win new business, the sales reps Tom hired were over-promising, committing to things that were never delivered. "Sure, we'll take care of that," seemed like a good response to customers asking for little extras during a project. While these promises were made with the best of intentions, they were not documented in the proposal process and the construction team didn't know about them until a customer complained.

As a result, customers were not pleased with the remodeling experience and they didn't recommend Tom's business to their friends and family. In fact, when asked about HomeScape, former clients were happy to share their irritation. Word spread, making it harder and harder for Tom to win new business in areas where his reputation preceded him.

Fortunately, Tom uncovered the real problem before it was too late. He updated his process for documenting client commitments and trained his sales team on how to effectively communicate with customers and record their requests.

The firm's service began to improve as these requests were tracked and delivered to the satisfaction of his customers. At the same time, potential revenue that was previously lost was recaptured through additional fees for change orders and add-ons to projects.

By its fourth anniversary, HomeScape Remodeling was generating lots of new referral business. Tom was able to cut his advertising budget in half and increased his profits dramatically. Solving the underlying problem instead of simply patching up the symptoms helped Tom build a more stable business, freeing up the cash flow he needed to continuing expanding.

The Symptom is Not the Problem

What can you learn from Tom's experience? **The symptom is not the problem.** If your business is not achieving the results you want, make a list of the symptoms you see and work backwards to find the source.

1. **Is business drying up?** It might not be the economy. Talk to customers and prospects—especially those that ultimately chose not to do business with you—to get their perspectives. Be sure you deliver on your promises and anticipate your customers' future needs and desires. You might discover that a competitor is deliv-

ering higher quality service or an innovative approach that is more favorable than your offering.

2. **Are you having trouble keeping good employees?** Set aside your ego and really listen to their reasons for leaving. Salary is often cited but is rarely the true reason for employee attrition. More likely, there is an issue with unmet expectations or a concern with a manager or supervisor that motivates key staff members to seek greener pastures.

   Research from the Saratoga Institute shows that 53% of employees leave for push factors such as a bad manager or poor company culture while just 10% leave for pull factors like a better opportunity.[2]

   If your employee turnover spikes, look to management or supervisors for potential issues (it might even be you).

3. **Is a price-cutting competitor eating into your market share?** They are probably not beating you on price alone. Figure out if the winning competitor has a better product or a more favorable customer experience by talking with customers about why they chose the other company.

   If you're not comfortable doing this reconnaissance on your own, hire someone to do a little research and report back to you on their findings.

One way to distinguish symptoms from problems is to make a chart separating the evidence from the cause. The following table shows some common examples of symptoms businesses exhibit when core functions are not optimized.

---

[2] Irvine, Derek. *Why Employees Actually Leave (Hint: It's Not Money)*. Compensation Cafe. http://www.compensationcafe.com/2013/01/why-employees-actually-leave-hint-its-not-money.html (accessed February 19, 2014).

Table 1

Symptom	Potential Problems
Good employees leaving	Company culture Poor management Competitive poaching
Customers not returning for repeat purchases	Disappointing customer experience Inferior products Unfulfilled promises Slow delivery
Lack of referrals	Poor customer service Missed deliverables Inferior products Unpleasant employees
Slow sales in spite of price cutting	Competitive issues Poor product quality Lack of market demand Delivery challenges

You can see from the examples above that a single symptom may have several potential causes. This highlights why it is critical to understand the forces that are really at work in your organization rather than assuming you know what's wrong.

Tackling the wrong problem won't alleviate an issue and it could even exacerbate the situation. Take the time to talk with employees, customers, suppliers, and others who may offer clues about what is really going on.

If necessary, engage a consultant or other third party to gather unbiased feedback and provide an objective assessment. A little extra investment at this stage can yield solid returns by accelerating a solution, taking employee emotions out of the process, and offering a fresh perspective.

Once you have a handle on the core issues facing your business, you are in a much better position to start looking for solutions. If there are several obstacles inhibiting your growth or blocking your success, pick the ones that will have the greatest potential upside for your company.

Don't try to solve every challenge at once. Decide which issues are most vital to moving your business forward. Address the opportunities with the most impact or the fastest results first. After you get a few wins under your belt, you'll gain the momentum you need to take on the rest of the issues. Remove those roadblocks one at a time until your path is clear.

Navigating Swift Currents

As I was watching the surf one morning on beautiful Kiawah Island, South Carolina, my mind drifted to metaphorical riptides and currents, and how they impact businesses.

Go with the Flow or Swim Against the Tide?

The expression "go with the flow" alludes to riding the prevailing currents. For me, this conjures up images of floating peacefully down the Chattahoochee River on an inner tube, enjoying the scenery on a hot summer day.

While that's a relaxing way to spend some leisure time, *going with the flow* is certainly not a proactive position for a business!

If you're just along for the ride, you might get lucky and pick up some unexpected momentum in your business. If the industry tides or economic currents are flowing in the right direction, they can help your business along.

There is risk involved in this laid-back approach. Why would you leave your business success up to the whims of the tides?

Of course, there are times when we need to coast, recharging our teams and ourselves after a big push to launch a product, win new business, or deal with other issues.

That respite shouldn't last long.

Allowing your business to go with the flow on a regular basis can be dangerous. When you set the autopilot, you could get stuck in an eddy or an undertow as you bob aimlessly along, losing market traction to more assertive competitors.

Fighting the Riptide

Sometimes market currents work against us. Riptides are an especially dangerous type of current that can sweep you out to sea when you desperately want to reach shore. Often and tragically, swimmers who don't know how to deal with a riptide drown from exhaustion as they struggle against the powerful current.

While rarely life-threatening for businesses, fighting against the tide can be difficult. Like a swimmer unexpectedly caught in a current they can't control, business flounders when you encounter currents you did not anticipate. As an entrepreneur, you're the navigator. It's up to you to quickly distinguish between a current that creates a positive flow and riptides that can sink your company.

Beneficial currents include things like technology changes that align with your new product strategy or changing attitudes that make your offerings more appealing to customers. These are the kinds of things astute executives watch for and capitalize on, jumping in ahead of competitors to take advantage of the turning tide.

In contrast, riptides lurk beneath a turbulent economy. They can manifest as rapid industry innovation that your company has difficulty adapting to, or even social media backlash resulting from poor employee judgment or unwelcome news.

Frequently, swimmers caught in a riptide give in to the instinct to swim against the current, fighting hard to break free.

Many executives also instinctively fight against the current, attempting to maintain the status quo or sticking to strategies that no longer suit the market environment.

When facing a riptide, the right thing to do is to move with the current, easing your way toward the safety of shore. For business leaders, this means first accepting the gravity of the situation and then rapidly acting to address it.

Instead of taking an intransigent stand, adjust your trajectory. Keep an eye on your goal and work with the current to get you there. You won't end up exactly where you set out to be, but you will be safe and your business will eventually get back on solid ground.

Untapped Opportunities

Opportunity is everywhere. You probably encounter people regularly who are full of ideas and suggestions for you, including well meaning friends and family.

The refrain starts with pleasant conversation over a nice meal or at a social gathering. Eventually the topic turns to business and you are asked, "How's it going?" You reply with a routine response, "Just fine, thanks." Then the suggestions start flying:

> "Wouldn't it be great if you could…"

> "You should just…."

> "I had a cool idea for you…"

The people offering these unsolicited suggestions may be sincere, wishing the best for you. Sometimes they simply need an outlet for their own entrepreneurial aspirations. Unfortunately, many of these ideas will not fit your business, aren't practical, or could even be detrimental.

Uncle Sal's latest suggestion might sound wonderful, until it ends up becoming a rabbit hole. Like Alice in Wonderland, you run down it only to discover later that you wasted scarce time and resources with zero return.

What you opt *not* to do can have as much or even more impact on the future of your business as the opportunities you choose to pursue.

Placing bets on the wrong option burns through precious time and money. You miss out on better opportunities when you're distracted by the wrong initiatives. "Opportunity cost" is the price you pay for choosing one option while foregoing another.

Understanding the cost of missed (or bypassed) opportunities in terms of unrealized revenue potential, loss of market share, or ceding a competitive advantage is essential to making sound business decisions.

Success in business requires the ability to find and evaluate opportunities efficiently, minimizing the waste that results from exploration without ROI (return on investment). Develop a filter through which you sift unsolicited ideas, as well as the legions of opportunities you discover on your own and those that bubble up internally through your team.

The ability to differentiate between viable opportunities and those you should let pass by may be the single greatest determinate of your long-term business success. This is a skill you must develop if you're not already adept at separating the two.

How do you avoid sacrificing the future of your business to an idea that is not destined to pan out? Can you learn to be decisive and act aggressively on opportunities that pay off big in growth and revenues without chasing a mirage?

The solution lies in adopting a sound strategy to guide your choices.

Charting Your Course

When you started your business, you probably took one of two approaches: you jumped in headfirst without thinking about a strategic plan, or you mapped out a detailed plan, possibly spending many months on the project only to find it went out the window as soon as it was exposed to fresh air.

The problem with most business plans is that they're just that: plans. By nature, they are based on what you *want* to happen, and reality often undermines that fantasy.

This is where strategy comes into play.

Do You *Really* have a Strategy?

In my consulting work I often find that executives think they have a strategy when they only have a plan. There is a big difference.

Strategy incorporates not only where your business is going, but also how you are going to get there. *How* is the tricky part, because it is easily confused with tactical activities.

If you think of tactics as *what* you do to implement strategic decisions about where to take your business and how to get there, the distinction becomes clear:

Table 2

Where are we going? (Strategic direction)	We aim to be one of the top three providers of avionics for commercial aviation.
How do we get there? (Strategic focus)	By leading innovation, bringing cutting-edge products to market faster than anyone else.
What will we do? (Tactical decisions)	Invest heavily in R&D, hiring the best and brightest from top schools, partnering with customers to anticipate their needs.

Strategy: Where you're going and how you'll get there.

Here's a scenario that illustrates the difference between strategy and tactics:

First, let's assume your personal **strategic direction** is "to live a long and healthy life."

Your *strategic focus* is on living well by eating a healthy diet and managing your budget.

This means when you need groceries, you'll typically decide to visit the nearest store and acquire what you want without spending too much.

Your *strategic objectives* are goals that support your strategy:

1) Acquire the groceries you need for the week, and nothing more.
2) Make the trip quickly and safely.
3) Complete your shopping efficiently and cost effectively.

Strategic decisions must be made to plan your trip in a manner that meets your objectives. These decisions address things like **transportation** (you'll drive and you have an efficient route in mind**), expense management** (keeping costs down so you can save money for something else), and **speed** (getting in and out quickly so you're not tempted to load up on extra goodies).

The outcomes of these decisions lead to **tactics**.

Table 3

Strategic Objectives:	Tactics Employed:
Get to the store quickly and safely.	Drive your own car. Take a familiar route. Obey all traffic laws.
Acquire what you need for the lowest cost.	Use coupons. Take advantage of "buy one, get one free" offers. Buy the store brand.
Shop efficiently.	Making a shopping list of the items you intend to purchase. Map your route through the store to avoid backtracking. Skip aisles you do not need to visit. Use cash instead of a check for faster checkout.

Tactics: What you do to achieve your strategy.

Your trip to the grocery store involves a number of tactical activities. These are the necessary steps to achieve your strategic objectives and execute your strategy: making your list, clipping coupons, finding your keys, driving, strolling the aisles, filling your cart, paying for your groceries, and making your way home.

Some of these items may appear to overlap. Table 3 illustrates the differences between them.

Another way to visualize the relationship between strategy and tactics is to see it as a process flow. Figure 1 shows how strategy can be broken down into components that logically lead to decisions on which tactics to adopt.

Figure 1: Strategy Map

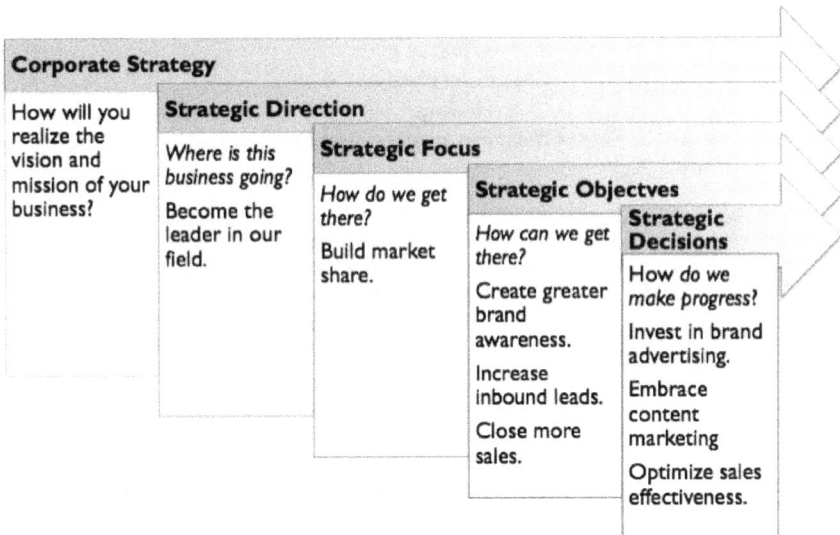

Corporate Strategy				
How will you realize the vision and mission of your business?	**Strategic Direction**			
	Where is this business going?	**Strategic Focus**		
	Become the leader in our field.	How do we get there?	**Strategic Objectives**	
		Build market share.	How can we get there?	**Strategic Decisions**
			Create greater brand awareness.	How do we make progress?
			Increase inbound leads.	Invest in brand advertising.
			Close more sales.	Embrace content marketing
				Optimize sales effectiveness.

People often get mixed up at the nexus of strategy and tactics. Tactical decisions are frequently referred to as strategies, as in "What's your advertising strategy?" or "We have a new product strategy."

If you think in terms of layers or levels, you can justify calling these things strategies. However, when you look at your business overall, a clear, top-level strategy that informs all these tactical decisions is essential for sustainable growth.

Figure 2: Tactical Planning

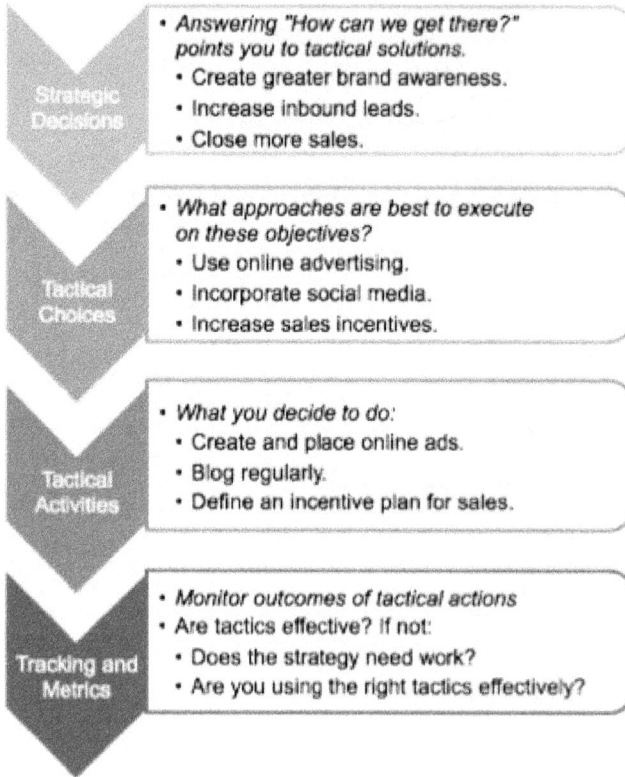

Strategic Decisions
- *Answering "How can we get there?" points you to tactical solutions.*
- Create greater brand awareness.
- Increase inbound leads.
- Close more sales.

Tactical Choices
- *What approaches are best to execute on these objectives?*
- Use online advertising.
- Incorporate social media.
- Increase sales incentives.

Tactical Activities
- *What you decide to do:*
- Create and place online ads.
- Blog regularly.
- Define an incentive plan for sales.

Tracking and Metrics
- *Monitor outcomes of tactical actions*
- Are tactics effective? If not:
- Does the strategy need work?
- Are you using the right tactics effectively?

Will Your Strategy Take You Where You Need to Go?

Now that you have a better understanding of the components of strategy, will yours take you where you want to go?

Did you dive into entrepreneurship without looking before you leapt? A few impulsive readers will confess to this, but most of you undoubtedly took the time to plan carefully before you launched.

As part of that process, you might have created a vision and mission statement for your firm. In fact, like many well-intentioned executives, you may have invested countless hours, and possibly thousands of dollars, in the development of these two items.

When all was said and done, what happened?

Did you invest extensive time and effort, polishing picture-perfect vision and mission statements to be proudly mounted on the wall, but no one reads them? Or were they stuffed in a binder and forgotten?

Let me challenge you to go back and review what you came up with. Is it still valid? Realistic? Does your vision and mission provide a solid foundation for your strategy?

The point of business strategy is to move you closer to realizing the vision and mission you set forth for your company. Not the carefully selected words, but the spirit behind them. If what you have in hand today is not strong enough to guide you toward fulfillment of these ambitions, it is time to revisit these core philosophies.

Strategy should not be intimidating, nor should it take months to define. As you can see from our earlier grocery-shopping example, if you know where you want to go and why, you can quickly formulate a strategy to get you there.

The same holds true for your business. Keep it simple.

Strategy exercise

Here's an easy exercise you can use to quickly create a strategy that works. Start by answering these questions:

1) Why did you start this business? What was the mark you wanted to make in the world?

2) Five or ten years from now, what impact will your business have had on the industry landscape?

3) What underlying factors (such as profit, sense of purpose, product, technology, etc.) have the greatest impact on your business decisions?

4) What do you want to achieve in your business over the next 12-24 months?

5) What are the five most important things you must accomplish to fulfill the goals you listed in Question 4?

6) What three obstacles or issues must you avoid in order to meet your objectives?

7) What primary actions and activities will you undertake in the coming year or two to further your goals?

8) How will you know you've achieved what you described in Question 4? (List three ways you'll know.)

Use your answers to complete the table below:

Vision	From your response to Q1:
Mission	Q2:
Strategy	
Decision Drivers	Q3:
Goals	Q4:
Objectives	Q5:
Road Blocks	Q6:
Actions	Q7:
Metrics	Q8:

This is the framework for your strategy. Add the answers to a few more questions, such as who your buyers are (customers), what you sell to them (products and services), and how they buy (your distribution channels and pricing models).

Plug this information into a one-page Business Plan Summary worksheet like the one at the end of this chapter, and you'll have the basic strategic framework you need to make effective decisions.

Persistence Pays

Even when you have a solid strategy, it's easy to get lost in the daily details of running a business. There's always a pressing need for your attention. From dealing with customer concerns to making sure new products get out the door, what needs to be done "now" can easily derail your vision for the future.

When you live in the moment—as many business owners do—it is not unusual to wake up at some point in time and ask, "*What happened?*" Where did the year (or quarter, or month) go? Moving from crisis to crisis may seem to keep your business afloat, but it certainly won't get you ahead.

Focusing too much on immediate operational concerns often means setting aside strategic intentions. The results can be disastrous to the health of your business. Think about the impact of more innovative companies on those that were standing still: Facebook vs. MySpace or Netflix vs. Blockbuster, for example.

You can't afford to lose sight of your objectives if you want to be successful in the long haul. But how can you balance today and tomorrow, keeping an eye on where you want to be while delivering on your current promises?

The annual strategic planning retreat is one answer. However, we all know what happens the week after, when the excitement wears off and the daily beast roars its head. Your best-laid plans end up on the shelf and it is back to business as usual.

Strategic management is not an annual planning event.

Business is a lot like sailing. In both endeavors, success is rarely a straight line. It's an ongoing process of navigation: plotting a course, checking your progress and adjusting as needed to get to your destination.

A sailor must actively account for changing conditions like wind, weather, and currents. Likewise, you must also use all the data at your disposal to make minor course corrections before trouble looms.

A good sailor will tell you to never leave the helm unattended because autopilot is a poor substitute for watchful eyes on constantly changing conditions. If you're too worried about fixing the broken latch on a hatch, for example, you might miss the sandbar ahead until you're hard aground.

As a leader, balance day-to-day trouble-shooting with a commitment to long-term objectives. Immediate issues will always need to be addressed, but this should be done in the service of your larger goals. To keep your focus on the horizon, translate your strategic plan into incremental milestones that will let you know you're on the right track, like mile markers on the highway or channel markers on the water.

Integrate your strategic objectives into daily operations and establish regular checkpoints to be sure you're staying true to the plan. Engage everyone in your organization to help keep the business on course, gathering useful information and sharing it in a way that can be acted on quickly when necessary.

Refocus Your Efforts

Have you realized as you read this that you are woefully off course? If you're not sure that your current strategy will support your business goals, use the worksheet on the next page to course-correct.

Track Your Progress

Strategic Objective	Actionable Goal		Mile Markers	Current Status	Course Correction
What "big picture" plans do you have for your business?	List 3-5 goals that will enable you to achieve each objective.		How will you know when you reach your goal? List metrics for each.	Where are you now? Have you started at all or are you still "thinking about it"?	If you're off track, what adjustments are needed to get back on course?
1		1			
		2			
		3			
		4			
		5			
2		1			
		2			
		3			
		4			
		5			
3		1			
		2			
		3			
		4			
		5			

Business Plan Summary

Vision

Mission

Core Values

Strategic Objectives

Target Markets

Primary Revenue Streams

Value Proposition

Unique Differentiators

Chapter 2

Prepare for Success

Is Your Business Off Balance?

When I was in high school I decided to take up dance. This was following a long hiatus after I quit my first ballet class in second grade. As a 15-year-old novice, I loved the movement and the excitement of dance, but I didn't have a clue what I was doing.

In my youthful enthusiasm, I failed to realize how far off balance I was until one day when we had a substitute teacher. As he was putting us through our paces he kept yelling at the class, "Find your center! Find your center!"

At first I was baffled, wondering what he was talking about. I thought, "Wow, this guy is in a really bad mood!" And then it dawned on me; he was talking about our center *of gravity*.

I never made it as a dancer but I did learn something important that day in class: there is no way to balance on one foot—or even two—without understanding at some intuitive level where your center of gravity is.

As a business owner there is plenty of pressure to be everything to everyone. If things aren't going well, we grasp at business wherever it pops up. We want our employees to be happy, our suppliers to value working with us, and our investors to be pleased with the return on their investment.

Unfortunately, dancing around trying to please everyone doesn't help you to be more successful. It throws you further off balance, often precipitating a painful fall.

Doing too much is like trying to balance on one foot without understanding where your center is. Just like a dancer, every business has a core, a center of gravity. It's the place where what you do lines up perfectly with what your customers need.

A client of mine once expressed his belief that, "If you try to be great at too many things, you end up being terrible at everything." There's some truth to that philosophy.

How can any one person or any single company fulfill every need, every desire, for every customer? It's impossible.

Even the largest conglomerate cannot accomplish this, and certainly a small business, solopreneur, or startup can't make it happen.

For your business to thrive, you must identify your sweet spot and make the most of it. Where is that center of gravity where you do your best work? What is the core from which you can extend your influence?

There will certainly be times when you are deliberately off balance as you stretch to achieve a new goal. Time can also have an influence on your sense of balance. As people grow from children to adults, our center of gravity shifts. The core of a business evolves as well.

Accomplished dancers can do amazing things. They appear to defy gravity, flying through the air and twirling in all kinds of unexpected directions. What to the casual observer seems like an amazing feat is actually an experienced professional using gravity to their advantage.

You can do the same in your business, providing you understand where your company's center of gravity is from day-to-day, month-to-month, and even year-to-year.

How do you discover where your center is? Here are three things that you can do to hone in on that precise point where you have the greatest impact:

First, look at the skills and knowledge both you and your company possess. What do you bring to the table that sets you apart? What can you offer that no one else can?

Next, consider your markets. Who are you selling to (target market) and who is your ideal customer?[3] These are the people who need what you have to offer.

Finally, consider delivery. How do you connect what you offer with people who need it? There are many ways to deliver products and services. What can you do to differentiate your customer experience and make it memorable?

Figure 3: Business Center of Gravity

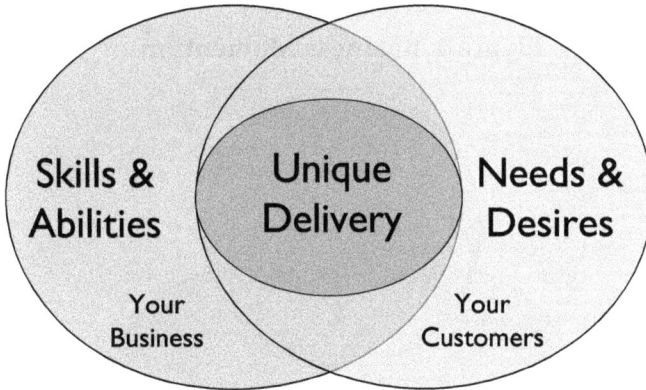

When you put these three things together, you'll get a good sense of where the center of gravity is for your business. It resides at the intersection between your abilities, customer needs, and the method of matching them up.

This is where your business should focus because it's the easiest and most compelling way to create success.

---

[3] To better understand the concept of an "ideal customer," see page 82.

Be a Pacesetter

Creating momentum for growth is a balancing act. When businesses get stuck, it's usually because one area or another is out of whack. Too much emphasis or too little attention on a critical area saps your velocity and sends your organization spinning out of control.

To avoid an unhealthy imbalance of focus, invest corporate energies in areas that not only drive momentum, but also propel your business down the proper path.

As I've worked with organizations to accelerate business growth, four different company personalities have emerged:

1. **Wanderer**: Likable but aimless, subject to whims of the crowd.
2. **Wallflower**: A best-kept secret, great, but no one knows it.
3. **Stuffed Shirt**: More talk than action, lacks a following.
4. **Pacesetter**: Magnetic leader with forward momentum.

Figure 4: Business Momentum

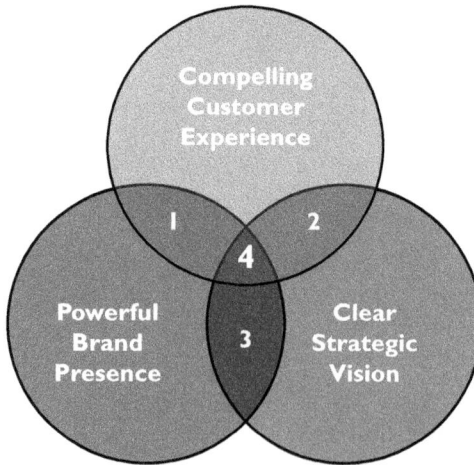

How do you know you're on the right track? The visual in Figure 4 should help. It shows the relationship between customer experience, brand presence and strategic vision.

Wanderers (1) are popular, but lacking clear direction. Because they don't have a solid or consistent strategy to guide them, they are easily swayed by the whims of the market.

Does a major customer want something you would not normally provide? Are you constantly chasing competitors? Do you find that your business runs in circles, no matter how much you aim to please your customers? You might be a wanderer.

Wallflowers (2) are smart but quiet. They know where they're going and how to get there. Customers quietly love them because they consistently deliver. Unfortunately, growth suffers because few people know how wonderful they are.

Being a "best kept secret" is not a growth strategy. In fact, it's a major liability if your primary customers exit the market. If this is you, it's time to start blowing your own horn and aggressively promoting your business.

Stuffed Shirts (3) are smooth operators. They're savvy and slick, knowing where they want to go and doing everything right to be visible in the process.

Unfortunately, they forget to listen to customer needs, charging ahead with their own vision regardless of whether it resonates with customers. As a result, their customer experience is less than satisfying, holding them back from reaching their goals.

Pacesetters (4) have it all. They balance strategic direction with customer focus and an appropriate level of investment in the brand. They promote their business, but not at the expense of positive relationships.

Strategic clarity helps Pacesetters stay on course, even as their momentum accelerates and business takes off. Competitors see them as the ones to watch, and customers will do what it takes to choose them over others.

Manage Your Momentum for Growth

We all need some time to kick back and relax, but taking it easy is not a great thing for your business. If your company's future depends on consistent growth, slacking off can have a negative impact on your prospects.

In business, there is no standing still. With the increasing angle of innovation, you have to be in constant motion just to maintain your competitive position, let alone move forward. If you plan to get ahead, you need momentum to carry your business through the inevitable ups and downs.

Momentum is not constant, it ebbs and flows like the tide. Sometimes it seems like momentum comes and goes from one day to another no matter what you do. Business challenges, like the loss of a key employee or an unexpected supplier problem, can spill the wind from your sails in an instant. Then just as quickly, you get a prestigious award or a big purchase order and all is right again.

When momentum wanes it can be hard to gather the velocity you need to scale the next big hill. Are employees burned out or budgets stripped bare? Without the power to weather the doldrums, one thing leads to another and your best-laid plans can quickly become unmet objectives.

Momentum Makes the Difference

The ability to manage momentum is a critical determining factor in which businesses succeed and which fail. Knowing when to hit the gas and when to ease up is as important as knowing where your business is heading. Even the best strategy won't see you through if you don't know when to invest or hire.

Do you hesitate instead of making an assertive move? Missing the market windows drains you of momentum, giving someone else an edge. At the same time, a rash decision can backfire if you fail to consider the full impact on your organization.

Look at business momentum like a roller coaster ride. Sometimes when you're working really hard it seems that you're moving so slowly that you will never reach the peak. In reality, your business is chugging slowly uphill with a purpose, gathering steam for the accelerated momentum that comes beyond the curve.

The hard work pays off once you get over the hump. Momentum increases dramatically as you scream downhill. On those days, the longed-for acceleration can be exhilarating—or frightening. You feel out of control because things are moving so fast and there's a temptation to step on the brakes.

The trick is to maintain control over both the direction and magnitude that create momentum. Stopping too soon will rob your business of the energy that is vital to starting the next big climb. An abrupt shift in direction to regain the perception of control can cause your business to get dangerously off track.

Figure 5: Momentum Cycle

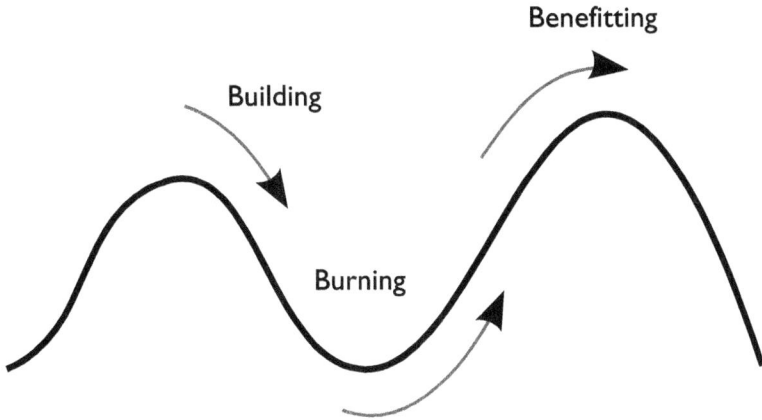

As shown in Figure 5, momentum gets you through the ups and downs of business.

Momentum builds during the chaotic out-of-control times when you're moving downhill so quickly that you can hardly enjoy the view. As you hit bottom, you lose momentum, burning through it to make the next uphill climb. And if you've managed it well, you've got the reserve benefit to move you over the next big hurdle.

Three Keys to Managing Momentum

1. Enjoy the ride when you have the opportunity, without hitting the brakes too hard. Keep the momentum going even when things are a little scary.

2. When times are good, don't coast too long or you'll miss out on creating the stored energy that's critical to keeping business going through the peaks and valleys.

3. Don't be afraid to use momentum when you need it to power through the tough times. You'll build more reserves later.

Get Rid of Your Ghosts

Lots of businesses have ghosts of things past that haunt them on a daily basis. In fact, there are probably a few ghosts or goblins hanging around your company. Even when you don't see them, they can hide in plain sight and hold your business back from reaching its full potential.

These are not real ghosts (if there is such as thing) but shadows of poor decisions, past employees, and customer relationships that died a slow painful death. The echoes of these events can color employee perspectives, inhibit even prudent risk-taking and undermine motivation.

Like most entrepreneurs, I'm an optimist and prefer to look on the bright side rather than dwell on the past. If you feel the same way, you may find it challenging to think about exorcising the demons you can't see when there is a new deal to chase or a fresh opportunity on the horizon.

Even so, it pays to take some time periodically to go ghost hunting and free your business from these pesky and potentially painful echoes of the past.

Things that can haunt your business include the lingering effects of…

- A bad-apple employee who undermined trust and disrupted your company culture.

- A poor manager who was divisive and created lasting walls between team members.

- A customer relationship that soured, leaving bitter feelings behind.

- A partnership that derailed, unraveling business opportunities and hurting revenue potential.

- Legal issues that contribute to a culture of fear and reduce risk-taking or innovation.

- Financial challenges that undermine investment opportunities and inhibit growth.

To get rid of these ghosts for good—or stop them from taking up residence in the first place—try this:

Discuss and debrief. When a business faces a setback, it is tempting for employees and management to deal with the issue by pretending it never happened. A healthier approach is to acknowledge the event with a debrief session that allows people to express their feelings and observations.

Sharing the impact of the experience allows people to unburden themselves rather than dragging extra baggage around and suffering from the excess weight they're carrying.

Learn the lesson and move on. Every situation holds lessons to be learned, but in the rush to "get back to business" it's easy to lose sight of them. Use your debrief sessions to uncover what was learned by your team, even if this process requires some probing, poking, and prodding.

Once you find the lessons, work on internalizing what you've learned so you don't end up stuck in the past, repeating old mistakes.

Undo the damage. Even after you learn the critical business lessons from these events, the damage can live on. Watch for ripple effects that linger. These may include subtle cultural shifts like hyper-conservative decision-making, employees fearful of retribution when risks don't pay off, or a general reluctance to stretch outside the norm.

If you notice your team is boxing itself in to avoid repeating a painful past, tackle the problem head on. Address the issue openly and encourage a return to a healthy environment.

Master the Art of the Rebound

When faced with a business setback, do you bounce back or just bounce? The answer is important, because mastering the art of the rebound is the key to resilience in business and in life.

We all have off days, even bad years. No matter how solid your strategy, how exceptional your team, how distinctive your IP, trouble is inevitable for a growing business. How we deal with it separates the leaders from the laggards.

Being resilient is essential to avoid a death spiral that can spell the end of your business. Those who bounce back most effectively not only have sound strategies for dealing with problems, they also have an innate ability to sense trouble before it appears on the horizon.

Part of this process is establishing good sensors that alert you to early indicators that the market is changing, a deal is going south, or a competitor is working on a game-changing innovation.

Assuming you have the tools in place to provide an early warning for approaching business issues, how do you address oncoming problems and respond in a way preserves future growth opportunities?

The resilience cycle in Figure 6 illustrates how an agile business anticipates major changes and leaps onto new growth cycles when the time is right. Wait too long and the crash becomes almost unavoidable. Leap too soon and you may abandon unrealized opportunities.

Figure 6: Resilience Model

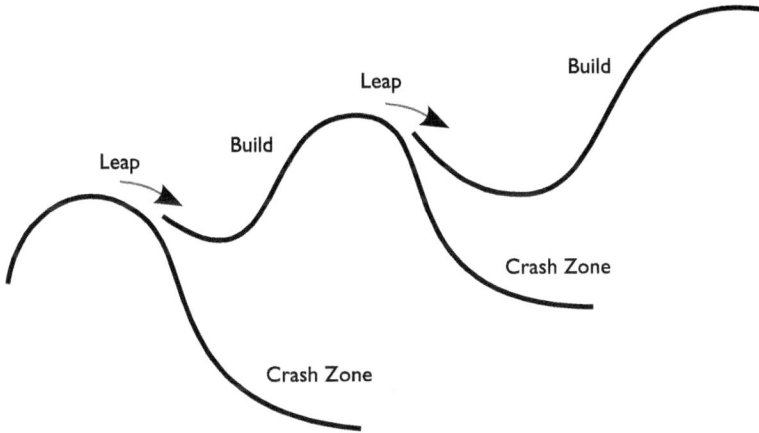

If you wait until after a crash to fix a problem, the climb back is like reaching the summit of Everest. It can be done, but few have what it takes to make it happen. The goal is simply too high. It requires time, conditioning, and capital that floundering businesses can't spare.

Any jump to a fresh growth curve includes a minor loss of momentum initially. This is to be expected as you gain your footing, become comfortable with the new environment and establish your new position. Don't let that early dip scare you unless it becomes protracted, which may suggest you chose the wrong path.

To avoid finding yourself in this position, plan ahead and practice making small leaps like these:

- When a product line shows signs of age, determine how to reinvigorate it or make the call to put it to rest.

- If a customer segment becomes unprofitable, seek out new markets and cultivate them before you need to rely on their revenue streams.

- When your employee pool dries up, work with local educational partners to develop new talent.

As these small leaps become ingrained in your company culture, it will get easier to make the call on big changes when necessary. The fear of the unknown becomes tempered by anticipation and excitement for the payoffs that your team has already seen are possible when embracing change.

Practice leaping a little every day and you'll learn to bounce back quickly when adversity strikes.

Chapter 3

Unstick the Sticking Points

Before moving on, I want to take a few minutes to discuss something that every business eventually faces. Sticking points are inevitable hurdles in your path. They're not signs of the end of the world, although sometimes it seems like they are!

At this point in the book, you may feel that you have lots of work ahead of you. Let me assure you that it is not uncommon to encounter points along your business growth curve where things seem to stall. You may hit a plateau after several years of steady growth, or you may be frustrated that your big plans do not materialize right from the start.

Don't get discouraged. This chapter is dedicated to getting you unstuck, so you can move on to bigger things.

Profit from the Plateau

I have a very successful client who hit the plateau in her tenth year of business. After years of steady, even award-winning growth, her business was stalled at a place where she felt that she was taking two steps forward and two steps back. After three years on the Inc. 5000 list of America's fastest growing companies, the business just wasn't getting any traction in the market.

While this is a common situation for many businesses, it was unfamiliar territory to my client. As a highly successful CEO, she was accustomed to delivering consistent growth year over year. Being stuck in neutral was uncomfortable, and she was anxious to get back into growth mode.

Lack of momentum in business can result in a crisis of confidence for leaders like this. Executives who are accustomed to seeing solid results may suddenly feel lost and indecisive, second-guessing themselves in their quest for renewed growth.

When you hit a plateau, you, like my client, may feel unsure what steps to take to get back on track. Don't let it get to you.

Sooner or later *every* business will be in a similar position. Growth cannot last forever and when it levels off, you may find yourself sitting on a plateau for weeks and even months at a time.

If you've been in this situation, you may recognize the signs: quarterly goals are missed and employees are unhappy. You're thinking about where to cut while wondering how to find a miracle cure for your business. It's hard not to feel like a downward spiral is on the horizon.

Before you panic, stop and consider whether this is a situation that requires immediate and decisive action, or is it a cue to take your business in a different direction?

Is the Plateau a Problem?

It's entirely possible that business stalled because you failed to anticipate a change in the market and customers got ahead of you. Customers outrunning the trajectory of your business create a momentum gap when their needs and expectations outpace your ability to deliver.

This can be caused when competitors or alternative solutions erode your growth, causing the growth curve to level out. It can also result when your focus wavers from evolving customer preferences, and their accelerating demands exceed your capabilities.

Figure 7: The Momentum Trap

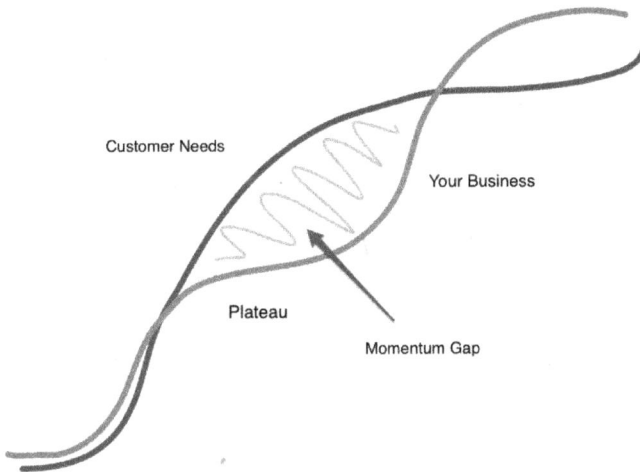

Customer Needs

Your Business

Plateau

Momentum Gap

To determine if you have a momentum gap, step back and do a little investigation before allowing knee-jerk reactions to interfere. If any of the following are true, explore further and reassess your strategy so you can respond effectively:

1.   A new technology is supplanting your current offering.

Think about the shift from DVDs to digital video as an example of how an evolving technology impacted a strongly entrenched business. Blockbuster and Netflix were both victims of slow response to evolving technology.

2.   A new delivery mechanism is diverting business.

Sticking with the example of videos, look at the change from rental stores to kiosks. Redbox was an early entrant here. Netflix, with its emphasis on home delivery, didn't consider the fact that some people prefer the experience of shopping for a video on a whim, without being tied to a monthly contract. (Netflix later regained its footing with on-demand services.)

3. Business is fragmented due to excessive competition.

In fields with relatively low barriers to entry, it is easy for competition to mimic your offer or to create an alternative that appeals to your customers. Local businesses like restaurants, high tech firms, and commodity offerings can all suffer this fate.

There is only room for so many pizza joints in a market, and the industry can only support a certain number of CRM solutions, social media management platforms, and online coupon services. When too many companies take a piece of the pie, the slices get smaller and smaller, leaving everyone hungry for more.

These are just a few examples. Depending on the nature of your business, there may be other factors like regulatory changes and economic indicators that cause business to stall.

Take a holistic view of your business that encompasses internal measures, traditional competitors, and market influences. Keeping a broad perspective enables you to avoid surprises by anticipating changes and responding before you hit a plateau.

Take Advantage of the Inflection Point

Pausing on a plateau is not always a bad thing. Incessant growth can cause fatigue. Battle scarred employees make mistakes and the stress can show in relationships with customers and co-workers. Sometimes, your team needs to rest and recharge to get ready for the next big push.

If you have ruled out problems such as those illustrated above, your business is on a natural plateau. Like the seasons of the year, there are distinct rhythms to growth patterns in business.

Cycles of rapid and slow growth occur as part of the natural progression of a business through its lifecycle. Learning to embrace these patterns gives you a competitive advantage. When you anticipate and prepare for these patterns, you can maximize the momentum they present.

Figure 8: Plateaus Along the Growth Curve

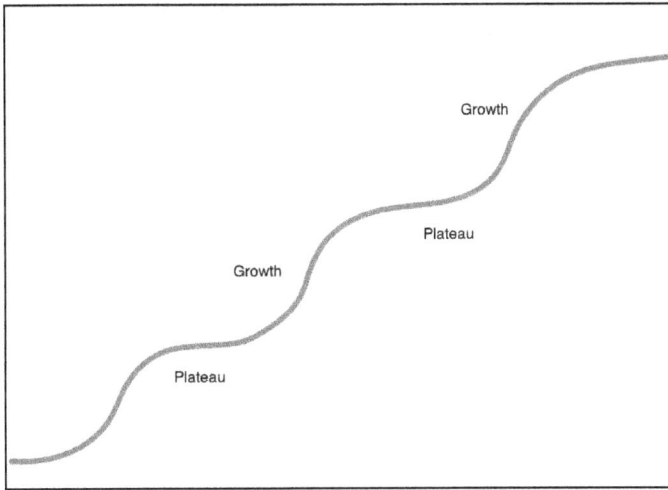

Think of your present position as an opportunity that will not last forever. Don't waste it fretting about what you could be doing or how things used to be better. Look at the plateau as a natural pause from the hectic pace of building the business. It's here where creativity and innovation blossom, if you allow.

Use this time to regenerate and store up energy for future growth. Catch your breath and think about what you've done right and where there is room for improvement. Recognize your team for their accomplishments. Reflect and evaluate your strategy. A little operational introspection can prepare your business for the climb to the next level.

Use your time on the plateau to plan for the future:

- Are there business opportunities right in front of you that you've simply been too busy to pursue?

- Is it time to make a strategic shift into a new market or prepare to launch a new product line?

- Are there aspects of your business (products, policies, or processes) that have run their course and need to be retired?

When you're in the fray, fighting tooth and nail for every new piece of business, these issues and opportunities can be easily overlooked. Now is the time to take in the view and see what you may have been missing. You just might find that your current vantage point exposes a path you did not see before. If so, make a plan and forge ahead.

No one wants to sit on the plateau for long. Business is meant to be dynamic and ongoing growth is crucial. Use the plateau to your advantage and instead of it becoming a dreaded flat line—or worse, the start of an endless decline—you'll look back in a year and realize it was the perfect place to prepare for your next phase of growth.

Are You Too Busy to Grow?

The opposite of a plateau is a business that is too busy to grow. I know that sounds crazy, but for many businesses it is true. It might be the case for your company as well.

Are you caught in a cycle of activity that makes it feel like you will never get ahead? Perhaps business is thriving, but you have no time to think beyond the here and now to plan for the future. Eventually, the activity trap will catch up with you and growth will stall.

This is a problem a lot of organizations face—and one I've been challenged with myself in running a business. Strategy and organization can easily fly out the window when you jump on a treadmill of *selling—servicing—marketing*. Add in product development, relationship building, and other "must do" activities and it can seem that there is never enough time to do it all.

Feeling Trapped?

In spite of the frustration and disappointment that comes with growing too slowly (or not at all), many business owners and executives do not even realize they're stuck in a vicious cycle of activity without momentum. They're overwhelmed, but fail to see the reality of the situation and how it is holding them back.

Businesses caught in this trap often exhibit one of these two key symptoms. Does either of these statements ring true for your organization?

You have a solid strategy, but don't effectively implement it because you are always dealing with more pressing things. Client requests, urgent appeals from partners, employee concerns, and competitive actions cloud your vision. The vague concept of "strategy" begins to feel less important than fighting fires.

You're so busy with everyday, tactical activities that you can't find time to plan. All the good intentions you had for mapping out a corporate strategy, a product roadmap, or your succession plan are sitting on the back burner waiting for the perfect moment when you're magically not busy. (*Guess what? That will never happen unless you close your doors!*)

If you answered "yes" to either of these questions, it is time to get out of denial mode and do something that will move your business forward.

Getting Unstuck

The symptoms of the activity trap appear in two opposing forms—either being stuck in first gear or racing so fast that you can't stop. Either way, the solution to getting unstuck is the same.

1. Commit to making a change

Getting from here to where you want to be is not easy, especially when the change involves choosing among several items you want or even feel you need to do.

If you are going to break the bonds of the activity trap, summon the intestinal fortitude to say "no" to some things in order to open up new possibilities.

Let go of activities, projects, commitments and customers that aren't adding value so you can focus on what is really important.

2. Give yourself breathing room

Many entrepreneurs equate being busy with productivity. They are *not* the same.

I know activity can feel like a safety net. It's discomforting to some people to stop doing things that have become routine. Seeing an empty inbox or a clean desk makes some of us squirm.

Get over it and take some time (ideally a full day, but a half-day or even an hour can help) to step back and assess how you invest your time.

Is email eating up hours of each day? Are you chatting on social media without getting results? Running around town for coffee meetings and networking events is only productive if they generate new business. If not, cut back.

Identify the areas that suck you in and make a few tough choices about what to give up. Delegate or outsource some tasks, and drop others altogether if they yield minimal return.

3. Look at the big picture

Now that you have opened up your physical—and mental—space to take a deep breath, step back and drink in the view.

Whether you have a strategy that hasn't been fully executed or you simply haven't taken the time to create one, contemplate where you're going. Where do you want your business to be next month or next year?

This step is not about spending hours creating a new strategic vision or writing up a long list of goals and priorities. It's simply a checkpoint: can you see where you're going? If you can't visualize your destination, you're not ready to move.

4. Get real

We all tend to kid ourselves about how much we can accomplish and how fast we can do it. Success requires realism as well as optimism, and you must be honest with yourself to break the activity cycle.

Once you know where you want to go, you'll see that there are certain things you absolutely must do to get there. We know intuitively that hitting a big goal requires completion of these steps, like executing on the strategy we mapped out for our business. *But that does not guarantee we do it.*

5. Set priorities

What's missing for many entrepreneurs is the connection between the big goals and the small choices that either move us closer to where we want to be or pull us off course.

Establishing clear priorities gives us a lens through which we can test our choices. Checking frequently to be sure what we *choose* to do is also the activity we *need* to do provides course-correction and focus.

Here's a simple way to balance your efforts:

Draw three columns on a piece of paper and make a list of things that you: 1) must do, 2) should do, and 3) want to do.

On the left, the **"must do"** items are non-negotiable. These might include paying bills and meeting new clients, but this column should also include things like building thought leadership through speaking and writing. Most importantly, it needs to incorporate the key tactical activities to support your strategic vision.

Your "must do" items should be planned out in advance as firm commitments. Build your schedule for items you "should do" and "want to do" around the must do items to ensure your most important priorities are met.

In the center, your **"should do"** list will consist of things that are important, but not critical to reaching your goals. These may be items someone else placed on your list, and you'll need to determine if their priorities are really yours as well.

Finally, your **"want to"** items on the right side can be used to fill in the gaps and add a little fun to your day. These might include updating the décor in your office, creating an extra piece of collateral, or sponsoring a charity event. (Of course, if that collateral is an important tool to help reach your goals, it should be on the left or center of your worksheet.)

Table 4

Must Do	Should Do	Want To
Complete tax returns	Look for a more affordable shipping provider	Attend a conference
Find a new distribution partner	Review resumes for interns	Volunteer for charity
Plan the product launch	Meet with a trademark attorney	Revamp the break room
Approve the earnings release		

If this little exercise results in a page that is too heavy on the left or has an endless list on the right, that's a sign that your priorities are out of balance. Work through each column and be sure you're being honest with yourself.

When you're done, you should have a much better perspective on where your time is going. You'll also see how time spent on less important tasks robs you of the opportunity to do more important (but seemingly less urgent) things.

Once you break free of the activity trap, you can move on to plan and execute a strategy that will get your business growing.

Finding Focus

With constant competition for our attention, focus is in short supply these days. From email bombardment to Twitter overload, endless meetings, and constant interruptions, it's difficult to shut out distractions and focus on the task at hand.

Are we losing our ability to concentrate on important activities because we are so conditioned to jumping from one thing to another? Is multitasking really anti-tasking because we never quite finish anything?

The Big Fizzle

A long time ago, I would marvel at how many things I could juggle, until I realized that items were dropping to the floor unnoticed! Eventually, I rediscovered those projects and thought, *"Wow, did I really never finish that?"*

How much time have you wasted on projects that get 70%, 80% or even 90% complete, but never make it over the finish line? It's probably more than you realize.

Based on observations in my client work, I believe this is a 21st century epidemic. It is exacerbated by the technology that was supposed to make us more productive, but actually causes us to constantly flit from task to task based on what catches our interest most effectively.

There's a lot of competition for attention these days, and it seeps into our businesses, draining focus and productivity when it is needed most.

Here's an example of what happens: You have a new project or program in mind and it starts off with a lot of excitement and energy from everyone on your team.

Pretty soon, other priorities chip away at the attention of key individuals, eroding enthusiasm.

Team members start to skip meetings. Deliverables are missed. People forget what the original objective was and the project begins to spin in circles—if it has any momentum at all.

The end result is a morass of wasted effort, distractions, frustration among partners and missed opportunities. Your efforts fizzle out and you wonder why you're not getting ahead.

This is not the way to run a successful business! It's time to break through the clutter and focus on priorities that matter.

Is that Urgent or Important?

The first step towards sharpening your focus is to understand the difference between what is urgent and what's important.

Urgent—must be done quickly

Important—must be done, eventually

This is a critical distinction because some things that are deemed urgent may actually be less important than other priorities.

Do you need to sign that purchase order for a fresh supply of pens? It's only urgent if you want them delivered tomorrow. Are new pens more important than reviewing the contract for a new copier lease? Probably not, but only you know.

Many of us fall prey to the belief that if we just take care of all these urgent little tasks, the distractions will go away and we can focus on the big important things. Unfortunately, there are always urgent items, minor emergencies, and fire drills to deal with, so we never get to the really important stuff.

The only way to find the focus you need to ensure success with those truly important activities is to first differentiate between the two, and then prioritize accordingly.

Many years ago I developed a simple rating system for projects that applies a matrix view:

1, 2, 3 ratings assess urgency

A, B, C ratings indicate importance

Using this approach, an A1 item is both urgent and important, so it takes precedence over an item rated B1 or A2. When something on my list scores C3, I need to question why it's there at all. Is it nice to have, or a waste of resources?

A1	A2	A3
First	*Third*	*Next Week*
B1	B2	B3
Second	*This Week*	*Sometime Soon*
C1	C2	C3
Today	*When There's Time*	*Skip It?*

Applying a scale like this to your to-do list ensures that important but less urgent tasks don't consistently land at the bottom of the list, where they languish for ages. Break big projects into small tasks and rate them appropriately so that important items get done.

Stop the Frenzy

Even with a system like this, you'll still encounter distractions that deter you from your goals. Overcoming that challenge requires the ability to block them out completely, at least long enough to allow concentration and creativity to bloom.

Sometimes this requires a change of venue, sequestering yourself or your team without email, cell phones, or media. It may be as simple as closing your door and turning off your computer for an hour so you can think. Taking a daily walk to clear your head can do wonders as well.

Breaking the frenzied cycle of activity—even for just a few minutes each day—allows focus and clarity to return. Making this a habit can help you and your staff develop the discipline to maintain attention on tasks that matter most to your long-term success, reducing missed opportunities and improving results.

Avoid Failure Work

A colleague of mine, Guido Quelle, uses the phrase "failure work" to describe wasteful rework that could have been avoided. Failure work includes correcting things at a management level that should have been done correctly at an operational level. It's an insidious drain on profitability and morale.

The best way to avoid failure work is to use tools like templated approaches, checklists, and other routines. Adopting these tools helps ensure that repetitive tasks and procedures are handled accurately time and again, instead of leaving operational excellence up to chance.

In the book *The eMyth Revisited* author Michael Gerber suggests creating a job description for every role you play. This may sound crazy to a busy entrepreneur, but taking the time to document what you do and how you do it can make things much easier when the time comes to hire someone to take over that task.

I've applied this in my own business for important activities that I don't do every day. From a checklist for press release distribution to a standard template for event marketing, I rely on these resources to make sure no steps are missed. They also make it easy to delegate tasks to subcontractors, interns, and new hires whenever necessary.

Another aspect of failure work is comprised of all those little irritants that you tolerate every day. Does it take three tries every time you scan a document? Do you spend an extra minute fighting with the lock on your desk because the key doesn't fit quite right? Do you have an older computer or other aging office equipment that consistently slows you down?

You may assume that living with these little annoyances and disruptions is simply a part of life, but it doesn't need to be. If you address these issues when they arise, fixing the problem at its source, you remove more than the irritant itself. You also avoid the distraction it causes, increasing productivity.

Surprisingly, the cost of such things is quite high. Research shows it can take several minutes for you or an employee to get back on task after pausing to deal with interruptions. These constant fits and starts can easily become a serial productivity killer.

The next time you catch yourself stopping work to fix a seemingly minor but recurring issue, address the root cause to prevent the problem from sneaking up on you again.

The Art of Stopping

What You Stop is More Important than What You Start

Are you always on the lookout for the next big thing? Where's that magic bean that will make your business sprout like no other? If you have not discovered it yet, feel free to keep looking. But I'd also suggest taking a moment to explore what's already in your storehouse.

How many programs has your company started that are not bearing fruit? Are you and your team wasting time on tasks and activities that provide no tangible impact on the bottom line?

When you make your daily to-do list or conduct your quarterly planning sessions, think about those items. What can you stop doing that will give you more time, money, and energy to invest in things that really do make a difference?

Focusing on the wrong things—especially tasks and activities that you've been doing for so long that no one can remember why they were started in the first place—can be a huge drain on productivity, creativity, and enthusiasm.

Watch for Stop Signs

Look around. Are you producing reports that no one reads? Are you running advertising but not generating high quality leads? Do you have daily or weekly staff meetings that are all chatter and no results?

Some of these activities need to be modified or even abandoned in order to improve efficiency.

How can you decide what to stop and what to continue? Take five minutes and make a list of questionable activities. If you're honest with yourself, you will probably come up with at least 10-15 items in this short period of time.

Keep in mind that just because you question an activity does not necessarily mean it is futile. Get input from your team to make the right decisions. You don't want to inadvertently disrupt processes that you are not familiar with if they do, in fact, serve a purpose.

Here are a couple of exercises to help you uncover the real waste in your organization:

First, ask your lowest-level employees what single task or activity makes the least sense. Is there something that has become standard operating procedure that seems incomprehensible to them?

To encourage candid responses, you might ask people to submit this information anonymously or keep their immediate supervisors or managers out of the feedback queue (give them aggregated data so they'll still be in the loop, but not in a position to judge.). Once you have your list, move on to step 2.

Next, shake things up a bit. Gather key staff members or your executive leadership team (if you are a solopreneur, use your advisors) for a different kind of brainstorming session. Instead of generating all the *new* ideas you can think of, develop a list of items that should be discontinued. If you need a little fodder for discussion, share the list you gathered in the first exercise to spark conversation.

You might be surprised by what ends up on the **Stop** list. Some items may be incredibly obvious. Others will be unexpected revelations. Take a good hard look at your list, talk with your core team, and pick a few activities your organization can do without.

Like periodically purging your office of old books and papers, you'll find the process is remarkably liberating. Not only will you have more time for other things, you'll open up space in your mind for fresh ideas and innovative approaches to your business that you may never have considered before.

At the same time, your organization will benefit from reducing wasted effort and increasing productivity in areas that count. When employees see that you're abandoning the *"because we've always done it that way"* mentality, they will learn that it is okay to question why things are done a certain way.

Encourage staff members to regularly provide suggestions for process improvements and efficiency whenever they see "Stop Signs."

Chapter 4

Management Matters

Evolving from the idea phase of a new business to the reality of daily operations can be a tricky transition for entrepreneurs. Some people excel at creating concepts for new businesses, others enjoy taking an idea and bringing it to life, while still others thrive on developing an organization and growing it into a big, efficient machine.

It's unlikely that you have the passion for all of these things. What roles do you gravitate toward because they are the most comfortable? What do you enjoy most along this path? Is that the best use of your time, or a convenient excuse not to tackle tougher issues?

Figure 9

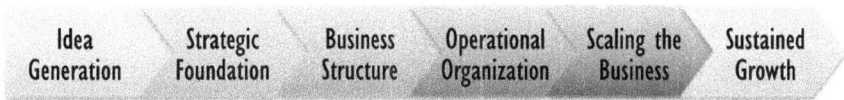

| Idea Generation | Strategic Foundation | Business Structure | Operational Organization | Scaling the Business | Sustained Growth |

Idea generators have great concepts, big ideas that can win the favor of venture capitalists and earn investment funding to give their idea wings. These are the Pied Pipers—the people who get everyone on board to make something happen. When it does, you may find yourself feeling a little restless, looking for the next mountain to climb.

It's OK to be an idea person (*a.k.a. a serial entrepreneur*), provided you recognize that is your strong suit. Go ahead, build your company and move on. On the other hand, if your desire is to build an organization for the long haul, you will need to learn to adapt. To be an effective leader and manager, you must deal with those things that are somewhat less appealing, or exit the business.

This chapter addresses ways to accommodate your skills and preferences so you can focus on what you do best. Focusing on the work that inspires you most will keep you energized and benefit your business, yielding happier employees and improved profits.

It's Not About Books

You do not need an MBA to be successful running a business. As one who grew up with more book smarts than street smarts, there were times early in my career when worldlier rivals ran circles around me. Eventually, I learned that the school of hard knocks delivers invaluable management lessons. No amount of classroom learning can replace the experience of getting down and dirty in the trenches as you fight for business.

It's a fact that some of the most compelling figures in modern business reached the pinnacle of success without the benefit of an impressive degree. People like Anne Beiler, co-founder of Auntie Anne's Pretzels, Larry Ellison of Oracle, and Richard Branson, founder of the Virgin Group, are just a few of the legions of successful business leaders who either dropped out of school or ended their formal education before completing college.

Books smarts don't hurt, but they certainly are not a requirement for becoming a savvy executive. Ideally, you'll develop both the formal knowledge necessary to be an effective leader, as well the knowledge that only comes from experience.

Know When to Let Go

While lack of a degree is a common thread among many entrepreneurs, there is another more important attribute that should not be overlooked. People who start businesses and build them into empires know when to get out of their own way. They understand their own personal strengths and weaknesses, and learn how to leverage their assets.

The leaders who are most likely to see their concepts bear fruit are the ones who sense when it is time to pass the reins and take action. They understand the importance of people who can put their noses to the grindstone and do the mundane tasks like planning and budgeting.

These entrepreneurs know the value of having someone on their team who keeps their feet firmly planted on the ground. Otherwise, the untethered foundation of their business may fly away like an escaped balloon.[4]

Good Advice is Priceless

Once you determine that you need to bring on help in various areas, make sure you get the best possible partners for your business. Whether you are hiring an entry-level employee or seeking out a CPA for financial advice, there is no room to cut corners.

High price does not guarantee quality, so shop around to find experts you can trust. Look for good partners who are both knowledgeable in their field and interested in your business. Be sure you can work well together, but don't worry about being friends. When it comes to hiring an attorney, accountant, or other professional, a healthy mutual respect beats friendly rapport any day.

The best time to hire an expert is before you need one. Ask colleagues whose opinions you value for referrals, then schedule meetings and establish a business relationship so there is no delay when an urgent issue arises.

If you do not already have a go-to list of providers for the following services, make it your mission to get them on speed dial in the next month:

---

[4] For a great example of what happens when a free spirit gets too tied down by success, read Inc. Magazine, *Inside the Mind of a Runaway CEO*. November, 2011.

- A general business attorney experienced in working with firms like yours, for assistance with contracts, agreements and other legal issues that will inevitably arise in the course of business.

- An attorney well versed in intellectual property (IP), trademarks and copyright law. Use them to protect your own IP and ensure you have proper permissions when using someone else's.

- A bookkeeper and CPA to handle taxes and financial matters if you don't have a CFO. Even if you do have accounting staff, a good CPA firm can be a valuable resource.

- An insurance expert to advise you on issues such as professional liability insurance, protection for corporate assets, business continuity and employee benefits options.

- A staffing expert or recruiter to help fill critical positions. Their industry knowledge and access to hidden talent can accelerate the hiring process and improve the quality of candidates.

- A human resources (HR) expert for staffing concerns, benefits, and employee relations. This person can help with sticky issues and keep you out of trouble.

Field the "A" Team

As you read this, you may have recently started a business with a core team of employees, or you might run a rapidly expanding company with multiple departments. Either way, the quality of your team should always be top of mind.

Regardless of what business you are in and how big your staff is, your people *are* your business. That's why the whole concept of "human resources" makes me a bit uncomfortable. The phrase suggests that people are resources to be consumed, that they are expendable commodities. That's simply not true.

The people who support your business as employees, contractors, vendors, and partners are essential to your success. These relationships are assets that require investment on your part, and can pay big dividends for your business. As with any investment, if you make poor decisions or risky choices about who to recruit or keep on your team, you stand to lose.

We'll spend some time here addressing people issues so you can field the best team possible. This means not only building an all-star staff, but also cultivating strategic relationships outside your organization.

What Skills to Hire

Certain skills like bookkeeping or assembly work may be viewed as commodities because they are repeatable, consistent processes. However, the people who perform these tasks are not interchangeable parts.

The question to ask yourself is, "Do I need these skills in house, or should I outsource?" Can a solid freelancer, service provider, or contractor deliver the quality and consistency you need? Is there a strong case for having someone on staff, either full time or part time?

How you acquire the skills and institutional knowledge your business needs is a critical decision. Bringing on employees is a complicated process that opens up a host of issues, from financial concerns to legal ramifications. When you consider making a new hire, the decision process should be well thought out and designed to foster success from the start.

I won't go into too much detail here because you can find a plethora of information and resources on staffing, both online and in most local markets. At a minimum, to make a successful hire you need:

- A clear job description and conceptual agreement on the duties and deliverables of the position.

- Realistic expectations about what can be achieved in this role, and how much to pay.

- An efficient onboarding process that helps new employees get acclimated quickly.

- Effective management with the ability to coach and train, as needed.

If you don't have these things in place or if you view a task as a commodity, it might be better delegated to an outsourced provider who will handle the people issues so you do not have to deal with them.

Table 5: Hiring Decision Matrix

Job Function:		
Decision Criteria:	**Yes**	**No**
We need this skill on a consistent basis.	Hire	Outsource
This position requires intimate knowledge of our business.	Hire	Outsource
Regular interaction with other employees is important.	Hire	Outsource
Talent is readily available in the market for an affordable wage.	Hire if you need someone with high employee interaction and intimate knowledge of your business.	Outsource to save money if you can use this skill on-demand (rather than full time).
This is a specialized skill that is hard to find.	Outsource if demand is sporadic.	Hire if needed regularly.
The position requires minimal oversight.	Outsource	Hire to enable greater supervision.
The person performing this function needs specific certifications or education.	Hire if you have a full-time need and can justify the expense.	Outsource if need is only part time.

For functions that require strategic thinking, judgment calls and creative input, in-house talent can be an asset, if you can afford it. As an alternative, a strong agency or consulting firm can fill the need more effectively at times. When you are looking for specialized skills that you only need on an occasional or part-time basis, outsourcing or contracting can be a good option.

Use a worksheet like the **Hiring Decision Matrix** on the preceding page to help you decide when to hire and when to outsource. Develop your own criteria to fit your business or use the parameters provided to make an assessment of which jobs that should be performed by staff and which talents to secure with outside help.

Dealing with People Problems

When I work with clients facing personnel issues, there are typically two types of problems: those that emanate from within the organization and those caused by an outside force.

The first is like a common cold: it affects you from the inside out. You get it because you have allowed yourself to become run down and your immunity is compromised. The second is more like poison ivy. It's the result of coming into contact with an external irritant that could have been avoided.

Different approaches are required to cure your organization, depending on the type of malady that afflicts your business. Just as vitamins and a healthy diet won't cure a rash from poison ivy, cultural changes or employee training will not cure an external irritant to your business. A proper intervention involves removal of the problem. Get rid of the offending weed, removing it from your corporate garden so you do not run into it regularly.

Systemic problems like a chronic cold need a more comprehensive approach. Changes in diet and lifestyle will improve your health so that respiratory problems do not take root and fester into pneumonia. Similarly, general malaise among your employees, infighting between departments, and lack of innovation are all problems that can only be cured from the inside out.

There may be structural or procedural issues at work, creating competition among employees for attention and resources. While some degree of tension creates positive friction, when things get out of hand, you must address the distraction by changing the way you work. Do you need better communication, more collaboration, or additional talent? Find the root cause of the problem and act on it quickly.

If you're struggling to figure out why things went awry, look to the top of your organization for cues about the source of the issue. You may have managers who aren't good leaders or unhappy executives who are poisoning the well. In fact, you might even be inadvertently creating the problem! Be honest with yourself. Are you are exhibiting behaviors you wouldn't like to see in your employees or promoting a double standard?

We're all human and there's no shame in recognizing that you have somehow caused a problem that needs to be resolved. The real shame is in not fixing it, so swallow your pride and move on. Employees will respect you more when you set an example by owning mistakes and addressing problems head-on.

Periodic Pruning

Successful businesses are adept at managing talent and anticipating people needs before they become a problem. To continuously move ahead, find the best people you can get and help them evolve with your organization. This may mean seeding your company with superstars who challenge everyone else to reach a higher standard. It may also require a little pruning of staff from time to time.

No one enjoys firing loyal employees, especially if they've been with you for a long time. When someone can't (or won't) keep pace with the organization, help them along the way by identifying opportunities for growth and encouraging their development.

Take a compassionate approach, coaching, advising, and encouraging employees into the best position for them that will also pay dividends for you. Sometimes this is a new role within the company, but often you'll both agree they need to move on.

When an employee resigns because they've tapped out growth opportunities at your company (or for any number of other reasons), support their decision to leave. If you've treated them well and helped them grow, they will retain an affinity for your business and can serve as an advocate from the outside.

At times you'll find your organization has outgrown the staff you first hired. Perhaps your Controller was great with the finances of a firm under $10M in revenues, but now you're at $25M and you have a new level of complexity that requires an experienced CFO.

Can you find suitable new positions for early employees where they still add value and find satisfaction, or must you part ways?

When it's necessary to give employees a nudge to move on, provide the resources they need to land on their feet. If they have performed well but no longer fit in the organization, offer outplacement services or introductions to others who can help with their search.

While the transition can be painful, these people will likely also become advocates for your business when they see that you have their best interests at heart.

Nip Problems in the Bud

The expression "nip it in the bud" refers to cutting off a flower bud to encourage healthy development. Removing new growth before it takes hold forces the plant to put its energy to more productive uses, creating a robust plant that ultimately bears more fruit or flowers.

This is also an appropriate euphemism for dealing with employee problems. Cutting them off when they first emerge allows your organization to thrive, reducing energy wasted on dealing with unnecessary disruptions and disputes.

A healthy organizational environment limits negative distractions and fosters positive interactions. The goal is not only a harmonious and productive work environment. Satisfied employees work harder and set a positive tone that is apparent to others inside and outside your company.

Customers can sense when employees are dissatisfied. Grumbling and grousing are bad for business. Even worse, disgruntled employees may deliberately sabotage your efforts to build a first class, customer focused organization. This can take many forms, from theft to deceit to open hostility or rudeness with customers.

If these issues crop up regularly, you probably have a systemic problem, which should be dealt with in the manner I previously described. However, if an egregious incident occurs with a single employee, act quickly to remove the offender. *Nip it in the bud* and get them out.

You must defend your business and rapid intervention is imperative. Problem employees rarely get better without significant effort. (Unless you are a therapist, you're not in that business.) Don't justify unacceptable behavior or make excuses for the inexcusable. Assert your right to have the best team you can, and when you discover that someone is consistently undermining that goal, they need to go.

If that sounds strident, it is. In my experience, managers know long before they take action that a problem must be addressed, but they delay due to fear of confrontation or legal recourse. I have seen cases where it is immediately apparent that a new hire was a poor fit. Unfortunately, instead of taking decisive action during the probationary period, the managers kept convincing themselves that things would get better. They didn't. In fact, as is usually the case, the problems were magnified through the lens of time.

In spite of your best efforts to screen for skills and cultural fit, this is bound to happen in your company sooner or later. Don't worry about diagnosing the cause. Until you've removed the problem, it is irrelevant whether the employee misrepresented himself or you didn't properly vet him. You can deal with that later.

Understand that a bad hire is a bad hire no matter how you look at it. The sooner you recognize and fix the situation, the better it will be for everyone involved, including the employee in question.

No More "Mini-Me"

The ability to recognize when you need to augment your own skills is a key success factor for your business. If you find that most of your staff are people you really enjoy hanging out with, there is a good chance you've surrounded yourself with people a lot like yourself.

People who hire on gut instinct are highly susceptible to "Mini-Me" syndrome. Of course you like that guy (or girl) you just met. If you went to the same school, your kids share a preschool, or you enjoy the same hobbies, that "fit" you feel is recognition, like looking in a mirror. And that is not always a good thing for your business.

Having too many people with similar personalities, backgrounds, or attitudes on your staff can result in paralyzing groupthink. Just because your team affirms a bad idea does not make it a good idea. Instead, it is a bad idea with traction, which can be incredibly dangerous to the future of your business.

To grow and stay innovative, seed your business with contrarian thinkers. These are people who challenge you to reach bigger, broader horizons. Look for people who make you just a little uncomfortable with their ideas.

These are not irreverent, obnoxious employees who contradict everything and refuse to follow the rules. You want team players that are comfortable enough in their positions to provide a little friction, because friction creates growth. (The pearl is a perfect example of this.)

How to avoid the mini-me management trap? Define the attributes that will make someone successful in a new position. Ask the right questions in the interview to determine whether a candidate has these attributes, and look beyond chemistry and gut feel.

While I do not encourage dependency on them, employee assessments can help when you're looking for diverse personalities or critical characteristics.

Tools like the Myers-Briggs Type Indicator and the DiSC personal assessment can provide objective measures of attributes that suggest an employee will be both a good fit for your company's culture and a high achiever in the role you need to fill.

There is a wealth of management assessments to choose from, and some are incredibly elegant in their simplicity. Culture Index is one such tool that I find both easy and accurate. Participants complete a short profile that quickly assesses their confidence, motivation and drive, allowing you as a manager to make smarter hiring decisions.

Get a Fresh Perspective

There will come a time when (if you haven't been there already) you have business challenges in front of you and you're not sure what to do. It happens to every business leader. That's why legions of professionals hire consultants. Rather than being a sign of weakness or inefficiency, knowing when to bring in outside help is a hallmark of an executive who knows how to get things done.

If you're not sure how to tell when the time is right to invest in consulting services, here are a few situations in which a consultant can help overcome business issues:

Expertise is needed. Does the consultant possess knowledge or skills that do not exist inside your organization? If you have access to internal resources, it could be better to use them rather than pay an outsider who does not know your business as well, for advice, unless:

1. **You need an objective view.** You might already have a strong opinion about what track you should take. Whether your assessment is based on facts or instinct, sometimes you need an objective third-party to validate your assumptions.

   This can be beneficial if you anticipate making a big investment of resources or capital, need board approval, or seek community buy-in for the path you plan to pursue.

2. **Speed or scale is an issue.** It's possible that your organization has all the talent you need. You could do the project, but should you? Is it a good use of your internal resources?

Maybe it is better to keep your team on task and bring in a consultant to provide focus (no competing priorities), scale (more people), or speed (doing in a month what would take your team six months to complete).

3. **It's time to shake things up.** No matter how smart you are, sometimes an outsider can see things you can't. Whether you need to reassess the make-up of your marketing team, reinvigorate your strategy, or prune your product portfolio, a consultant can help.

   As objective advisors, consultants view your business without the filter of emotional attachments, helping identify weaknesses or opportunities that may have been obscured by your firm's tradition, culture or habits.

4. **Stealth or anonymity is required.** In certain cases, having the work done by someone at arm's length to your organization is best. If you are collecting competitive information, looking for leaks in your own company, or exploring potential partners, suitors, or acquisitions, a consultant can be the right choice.

   Experts can often find information that is not readily available to your or your team and can gather sensitive data without stirring things up.

Find the Right Consulting Partner

Hiring a consultant is a risk. It can pay off in spades or cost you money and time if the results and advice aren't what you need. So how can you tell if a consultant is right for you?

I spent over 20 years in the corporate world working for very small businesses and massive firms like UPS. During that time, I interacted with different types of consultants on a variety of projects. Some of these I hired personally, others were engaged for projects that touched my domain. In most cases, these projects were successful. Other times, things just didn't work out.

No one plans to hire a consultant for a project that fails, and consultants want to be successful just as much as you do. Most of them realize that the happier their clients are, the more likely it is that they will be invited back for a return engagement.

Consultants also know that referrals—the lifeblood of their business—depend on maintaining a sterling reputation. You should expect that the consultant you bring on will have your best interests at heart, working hard to deliver the results you need.

To ensure that your project works out as planned, here are few things to keep in mind when hiring a consultant:

Does the consultant have the right expertise?

Just because a consultant did a great job for someone you know does not guarantee they will be the right fit for your organization. Ask them about their knowledge and experience in your industry. Find out about work they've done with companies of a similar size. Have they addressed business challenges that parallel the problems you are facing?

A good consultant should be able to provide concrete examples to demonstrate their expertise as well as their suitability to work with your company.

How deep is their knowledge?

The search engine optimization (SEO) field is a great example of an industry that spawned thousands of "experts" without much evidence to prove their worth. When SEO first became a must-have for any business with a website, anyone who knew a little about the topic could hang out a shingle and call themselves an expert. More recently, social media became fresh and fertile ground for a new round of faux experts.

Whatever the specialty, when it comes to consulting, "buyer beware" is good advice. That's not to say that there aren't plenty of highly qualified professionals out there. There are. The challenge is finding them.

If you are considering investing in a professional to help you with any issue you do not fully understand, you could easily become the unwitting victim of a well-meaning but not well-trained consultant.

To avoid this problem, ask for references and check them. Be sure the contacts you are given are not the friends, relatives, or business partners of the consultant in question. When you call to verify references, ask questions like:

- What kind of results did you get? Were they what you expected?

- Were you satisfied that the consultant was knowledgeable and proficient in the skills needed for the engagement?

- Would you hire this consultant again? If not, why?

Will you work well together?

You do not need to become best friends with your consultants. In fact, a little professional distance can be healthy so don't hire a good friend or your brother-in-law.

The quality of your working relationship plays a big part in the success of any project, so it pays to think about the chemistry between you or your team and the consultant you're considering hiring.

What should you look for? Communications style is a good place to start. Do you want someone who is blunt or direct in his or her feedback, or would you prefer a softer approach? What about written communications? Do you expect a detailed written report every week or would you find a simple summary presentation more palatable?

> **A Little Tension is Good**
>
> While it's nice to work with people we like, finding a consultant you respect is more important.
>
> Don't worry if there is a little "constructive tension" as they push you outside your comfort zone. That can be a good thing.
>
> Often transformational change requires abandoning safety and reaching further than you previously thought possible.

How about their approach? Are you looking for someone who will spend lots of time with your team, jointly probing problems and opportunities? Would you prefer someone who does an initial assessment, then disappears until they are ready to return with the answers in hand?

Maybe your team needs a collaborative approach with input and engagement along the way. If regular check-ins and status reports are important, make sure that is clear. If a hands-off approach better suits your style, clarify that as well.

Take some time to think about your current organizational culture and your personal work style. Look for a consultant that can complement—rather than conflict with—your approach.

Getting Results

In the end, results matter more than anything else. If you are getting ready to spend thousands of dollars for a consulting project, you need to be comfortable that your consultant can deliver the results you expect. Do not assume that you will get a report like the one you saw from the last consultant, or that the work will be just as good, as detailed, or as insightful as you envision.

Prevent misalignment of expectations by discussing up front what you hope to achieve from the engagement and what the deliverables will be. Do you want a list of recommendations you can implement on your own? Are you looking for a detailed action plan? Do you expect the consultant to help with implementation? Address these items before you sign an agreement.

Who is doing the work?

Many large consulting firms send in the big guns to close the deal, and then assign junior staff to do the real work. If you are paying top dollar for the expertise of the principals of the consulting firm you hire, make sure they will be working on your project. You might even ask for this in writing.

With smaller firms, there are two business models to consider. Some have full-time staff to handle various aspects of their consulting engagements. Other firms scale virtually, bringing in talent as needed. Both approaches have their own benefits and drawbacks.

Existing staff can be an advantage with a highly focused firm where employees work on similar projects, one after the other. They build a base of experience that can be beneficial for your engagement. The downside is that you are more likely to get a cookie-cutter approach to problem solving, with advice that echoes recommendations given to other clients in similar circumstances.

You will also work with whoever happens to be on staff, whether or not they are the best fit for your specific project. The firm has an incentive to utilize their staff as much as possible to get a return on that investment. You may discover resources added to a project that could have been handled by a smaller team. Be mindful of "team bloat." If budget is an issue, insist on a lean and limber team.

A firm that scales virtually has the luxury of accessing talent on demand to meet very specific client needs. They can find the right expert for your project instead of forcing a fit with someone on staff who may not have the precise expertise the project requires.

When selecting a firm that uses this approach, make sure they have strong relationships with a broad selection of experts for various projects so they can field the right talent at the right time.

How objective is your consultant?

A final word of advice: find out if your consultant is beholden to anyone else. It is not uncommon for consultants to affiliate with business partners in exchange for a share of revenues. This practice is perfectly acceptable, if it is disclosed. To be sure, ask.

If you are hiring a consultant to help you find a web hosting company or to create a digital media strategy, for example, they may have affiliate relationships in those areas. Likewise, a consultant may earn a referral fee, markup, or commission for assessments and software they recommend.

Will they be able to objectively propose the best solution, or will their recommendation be for the company that pays them? If you're not sure, ask.

Building Your Advisory Board

Regardless of whether you're running an early stage startup or have been in business for several years and whether or not you have a board of directors, an advisory board can provide the extra support and expertise your business needs.

An advisory board can be beneficial even if it comprises just two or three people. The advisors can be extremely helpful to a very small company, providing experience-based guidance and essential business connections to move your company into the next phase of growth.

If your start-up is pre-revenue or your business is still in the planning stages, it's not too early to think about who your advisors might be. Rather than waiting until some undetermined future point when you are "big enough" to need one, start assembling an advisory board at the point when your business plan is coming together.

An advisory board can guide you through critical decisions in these early days, avoiding costly mistakes with the potential to hurt your business later. A young business with an advisory board can also benefit from board members serving a marketing function, spreading the word about your business to their friends and colleagues. *(This is a benefit for more established businesses as well.)*

Can You Take Advice?

If this all sounds good and you are eager to create an advisory board for your business, there's one more essential step before proceeding. As a checkpoint, ask yourself, "Are you really open to the input advisory board members will provide?"

The intent of creating an advisory board is to solicit feedback and advice from experts who have walked in your shoes. To be successful, you should be open minded and willing to consider advice from other professionals. If not, the exercise will be a frustrating waste of your time and that of your advisors.

If you prefer to keep your own counsel, skip this step, but realize that you have a business handicap: no one knows *everything* they need to know to run a successful business.

Pick the Right Advisors

Once you have decided that it is time to form a board of advisors, you need to find the right people to join it. Not knowing who makes a good advisor and who to include or exclude is a concern that stops many business owners from creating an advisory board.

It's true that wrong choices can backfire with misguided advice or inappropriate interventions. If you're savvy about the process, you can, and should, establish a board of advisors to accelerate your growth and improve business results.

> Having paid legal and financial experts on call is mandatory. Don't rely on free advice in this area—you'll get what you pay for!
>
> Build relationships with professionals you can trust and call on them whenever necessary.

Ideally, start by finding someone to serve as a generalist advisor who has a successful track record of building companies. Consider this person the anchor on your board and add skill-based advisors to augment your professional, financial, and legal team.

When choosing advisors, look for passionate people who "have your back" and will be straight with you. These people do not need to be friends or even current business associates. In fact, people who know you too well might not be the most objective advisors. Look for people one or two steps removed from the inner circle of your business network. Instead, foster new relationships to expand your reach and maintain objectivity.

Look at your current team, both inside the company and on your existing advisory board, if you have one. Think about gaps and deficiencies and fill them with advisors who have skills in those areas. You might need someone who can provide a high-level view of strategy, target markets, and business model options. These people will pull you out of the weeds, forcing you to think about the business at a higher level.

Expertise in your market or industry is not the most important factor in selecting an advisor. At the executive level, key skills are highly transferrable. Seek out advisors who know your target market well, even if they are from a different industry. Advice from an outsider who provides a fresh perspective on a particularly troubling issue can accelerate your business faster than the tried and true approaches of an industry insider.

Recruit the Best

To build the best advisory board for your business, do not be afraid to seek out someone who you believe would make a good advisor for your company, even if you do not know them personally. Be strategic in your choices. Identify holes in specific skills, knowledge, and talents. Do you need input on marketing, finance, or product decisions? Identify people with expertise in these areas.

Ask people in your network or professional advisors like your accountant or attorney for recommendations to address your specific needs. Once you get an introduction, schedule a meeting or coffee to get to know this person. Tell them what you need and why you would like them to work with you.

As you talk with prospects about joining your advisory board, let them know about the expected time commitment. For a potential advisor it can be very helpful to know things like, *"We have quarterly meetings in Atlanta, with dinner the night before. Then we meet the next day from 9am – 1pm."*

Particulars like this can sway a decision one way or another and being open ensures that you'll find a good fit. Don't worry if you get turned down a few times. Many executives are looking for board experience and are open to helping developing companies, so you should not have much trouble building a solid advisory team.

Making it Work

Once you have your advisory board in place, you want to get the most from this valuable asset. Be intentional in your approach to utilizing your advisors and be respectful of their time and contributions.

When you meet with an advisor, put specific parameters around your demands on their time. Let them know, "I need an hour (or a lunch, a short call, etc.) to discuss _____ topic." That way they know what the time commitment is, and what you need and expect from them.

Use advisor's time wisely, be gracious, and openly communicate successes and challenges so that your advisory board members feel both valued and connected to your business.

When to Meet

It's wise to create an environment where your advisors can get to know each other, in addition to the one-on-one meetings you may have with individual advisors. Regular meetings of the group build rapport and facilitate the board working well together. Aim to hold group meetings at least a couple of times each year.

Think about what you want help with before getting together, and do not meet just for the sake of meeting. Use the board to address your business needs, not your advisors' personal wish lists, which may be very different from your own.

Prepare an agenda that addresses your challenges and the kind of input you need, and make sure that is the focus of your meeting. Sending the agenda in advance, along with any references or reading materials you want to discuss, will make your time together more productive.

Don't feel obligated to do everything your advisors suggest. When advisors have their own vision or agenda for your business, be careful about being sidetracked and losing sight of your strategy. It's your business, and you're the one accountable for evaluating the advice you are given.

You can't—and don't want to—follow every piece of advice you're given. You risk getting whiplash if you change course every time you encounter a fresh opinion, especially when your advisors have vastly differing perspectives. Consider the advice, then decide on your own terms what to act on and what to disregard.

Structure is a Good Thing

Putting a framework around meetings and creating a structure for your board of advisors with things like a time limit on board service (1-3 years) can be beneficial. This way, you can set expectations and bring on fresh talent to gain new perspectives when you need them.

A structured approach forces you to be both organized and intentional. You will need to prepare for board meetings, getting materials out in advance as you would for a meeting with your board of directors. This makes you more prepared and helps your advisory board be more productive.

While structure can help your board function more smoothly, there's no need to be rigid. You may choose to have occasional one-on-one meetings with advisors to address specific needs or concerns, especially if you need to "go deep" into an issue.

Keep in mind that unlike a board of directors, your board of advisors works for you. If things are not working out, you can (and should) replace ineffective advisors with more suitable ones.

At the same time, remember that advisory board members are not your employees. Don't ask them to do things like build your website or research a market for you. Remember, your relationship is about getting guidance, not free work.

Your advisors are voluntarily contributing time to your company, so it is important to show your appreciation. Compensation isn't necessary, but recognition of your advisors' contributions is considerate.

Steer away from monetary compensation or equity for advisors who are already successful in their own right. They are helping you because they are passionate, not for the financial gain.

It may sound like a good idea to offer advisors equity in your company. However, if you choose to do so, remember you can't get it back later on if things don't work out. A better way to show appreciation is to make a donation to a favored charity or host an annual event or outing for your advisors to enjoy.

Averting Disaster: Beyond "Plan B"

Every few years an event like a major hurricane blows by, reminding businesses to check their disaster recovery plans. When the last major storm appeared, you might have pulled out your own plan for review. Maybe you were unprepared and simply thought, *"We really should have an emergency response plan."* If so, you're vulnerable and it's time to take action.

Think about it. What would you do if your company lost a week or two of productivity? Could your business survive? This may sound extreme, but the reality is that it's not uncommon for businesses to be hit with unexpected interruptions due to natural disasters, fire, water damage, power outages, loss of a key executive, and other factors beyond our control.

Most business owners make big plans, and they anticipate the "what ifs," so they can sleep well at night. That's fine…until everything falls apart because something was missed or someone assumed—in error—that a certain back-up plan would work. In these situations, the basic "Plan B" contingency plan doesn't cut it.

When Plan B fails, we're left with two choices: the worst-case scenario is to give up and go home, or we can forge ahead and make the best of things. To make the process of moving forward a little easier, here are a few things to think about:

Do you have an alternate plan to keep your business running when things go awry? In the case of a fire, snowstorm, earthquake, or other catastrophic event (perhaps a zombie attack?), can your employees work remotely from home or a back-up location? Are your files accessible from the cloud? Can your systems be restored from an alternate location or a contingency provider?

If you were to lose a major product or service offering, do you have something you could sell in its place? Suppose a component of your core product was recalled or became unavailable? What would you do? Having another option can keep revenue coming in while you deal with the issue.

How will you cope with the loss of a key employee? We hate to think about it, but life happens. People quit, get sick, and sometimes pass away. Don't be complacent and put all your faith in one indispensible employee who knows everything. Cross train staff and capture institutional knowledge so business can keep running smoothly without key players.

If your best customer pulled the plug, would you have others to take their place? If you get more than half your revenue from one customer, start looking for ways to generate new business. If that single customer were to suddenly shut down or take their business elsewhere, how would you replace them?

The Personal Side of Disaster Recovery

Most standard disaster response plans cover things like how to maintain ongoing communications and sustain operations, addressing questions like:

- Where will our temporary offices be?
- How will we communicate with employees?
- What will we say to the media (and on social media)?
- How do we reroute the phones?
- What will we do about inventory losses?
- Can we continue shipping product or delivering services?

If this sounds like your plan, you are missing one really important element: **people**.

As a Florida native, I'm a veteran of many hurricanes, most memorably Hurricane Andrew. In August 1992, I was five months pregnant, living just south of Miami and had recently purchased my first house. Six weeks later, Andrew destroyed that home along with those of most of my friends and co-workers. Andrew also devastated large numbers of businesses, ruining property and scattering employees.

In the days after the storm, my friends and neighbors rallied together, sharing tips on how to get through the insurance mess, where to do laundry, and how to send mail. Thankfully, my employer did not care that I showed up for work in dirty shorts and a ragged t-shirt (most of us were equally dirty and not exactly shower-fresh).

Although it took months to recover, my employer and my family got through the mess. We all learned some valuable lessons in the process. Here are a few points to consider for your own contingency planning:

How will your employees get to work if there is a natural disaster? Simple things like commuting to work become a real problem when your car has been destroyed and there are no buses running. One solution is to offer employees transportation through ride sharing or a company-run shuttle.

Can you accommodate flexible hours? What will you do when employees need time off to meet with the insurance adjuster, deal with emotional trauma, and pick up the pieces of their lives? Consider allowing employees to shift hours as needed, and relax requirements for using paid time off.

What about housing? In a widespread disaster, many employees will be forced out of their homes. For homeowners, insurance may provide an allowance for temporary living expenses i.e., renting an apartment. However, housing and furniture will likely be in short supply.

Employees without insurance won't have a safety net. They could be forced to live with relatives or to leave the area altogether. If employees relocate, even on a temporary basis, they may experience financial strain from acquiring basic necessities or managing a long commute.

How will you replace employees that leave and never come back? This was a big issue after Hurricane Katrina, since so many people were out of their homes for an extended period of time. Some decided it was easier to resettle in another city than to come back and rebuild. Can you retain employees through a transition time like this by allowing them to work remotely?

If you run a local business, the impact of a catastrophic event on customers is also a concern. Will they return when you reopen your doors? Plan ahead to stay in touch with existing customers to let then know how things are going and when you will be ready for business.

When disaster strikes, community counts. The ability to rebuild your business may depend on how you engage with employees and customers in the days following the event. Think in advance about ways you can support customers as well as employees in an emergency.

Depending on the nature of your business, you may be able to offer free products or discounted services to the local community. If that is not an option, think of ways you can help by providing access to meeting rooms, sponsoring meals, or other services.

A little goodwill can help speed the recovery process and it will be remembered for a long time.

Chapter 5

Key Strategies, Critical Choices

Reassess the Competition

Are you confident that you know your competition, or do you just think you do? There's a common affliction among executives, especially entrepreneurs who are working on *the next great thing* to claim, "We don't have any competition." Even when there is an awareness of the presence of competitors, the view can be myopic.

Maybe your product *is* the coolest thing since sliced bread, but that does not mean you don't need to watch your back. As the Joseph Heller said in Catch-22, "Just because you're paranoid doesn't mean they aren't after you." Competition is everywhere. So stop and think for a minute, do you really, truly understand your competition?

Competition Is About Choice

Assessing your true competition is a matter of taking stock of choices. What alternatives do your customers and prospects have when tackling the problem you solve? The answer is not only other companies that do what you do. There are more ways to solve the problem, and other options for your prospects.

Let's look at the example of a carpet cleaning business:

Tom cleans carpets. So do thirty-two other companies in his town. A little quick math will suggest he has thirty-two competitors, right? Not really.

What about all the stores that rent carpet cleaning machines? Isn't Tom competing with Lowe's and Wal-Mart and Kroger and every other retail outlet that offers heavy-duty machines for homeowners to use?

Then consider home carpet cleaning machines. Certainly the DIY market cuts into Tom's business. If Ann has her own carpet cleaner, she's probably not calling Tom very often.

What about people who just never clean their carpets? Are they competition...or just lazy? The choice of doing nothing has a competitive impact.

Finally, do not overlook alternative flooring. People selling hardwood or tile are undoubtedly pitching customers right now on the fact that maintenance is easier and less expensive than regular carpet cleaning.

The Long View

Taking a broader view of the competition is essential to understand the true dynamics of your market. If it has been a while since you looked at your competitive landscape, you might be surprised by what you find.

Here are four considerations to keep in mind when sizing up the players in your space:

1. **Direct Competitors:** companies that are in a head-to-head battle for your customer. They do what you do, in a similar way at a comparable price. For Tom, the thirty-two other carpet cleaners in his town are direct competitors.

2. **Indirect Competitors:** businesses that solve the same problem as your firm, but in a different way. In our example, cleaning machine rentals and home carpet cleaners are indirect competitors for Tom.

3. **Alternative Solutions:** a choice that circumvents the need for your solution, like choosing hardwood instead of carpet.

4. **Inertia:** the choice to do nothing at all. People who never clean their carpets could be Tom's customers, if he could just convince them of the need.

Don't be complacent. If you are confident that you know all your competitors, consider for a minute the impact of Apple's iPod on the demand for music CDs (if you haven't seen a CD in a while, you get the point). How are print magazines doing in these digital days? Think further back…what happened to all the carriage makers after the car came along?

Every industry, no matter how solid, can and will be disrupted by new technology.

Get Ahead of the Game

You may not be able to stop the changes brought about technological innovations, but you can keep ahead of the wave by staying on top of competitive forces in your industry. Don't settle for simply watching your direct competitors to see what they do. That's like driving while looking in the rearview mirror and it could be the death of your business.

To stay healthy, take a long view. Look over the horizon, constantly thinking about what could be next. Is someone working on a better way to solve your problem? Is someone developing a way to make the problem go away or to prevent it altogether? Those are the people to watch.

Use Social Media for Competitive Listening

It's amazing what people share on social media, and not all of it is racy or inappropriate. People often post about routine work activities, not realizing that this chatter provides a glimpse into their company's strategies. You can use this information to your advantage if you know what they're saying.

When it comes to competitive monitoring, using social listening to hear what's being said in the public domain can uncover eye-opening information about your competitors' actions. Keep up with competitors by tracking their corporate and employee posts to learn what's going on at the company, such as potential partnerships, vendor changes, and key new hires.

For example, if you know Joe Jackson is a key account rep at Widgets Express, you might be interested to see he has recently connected with the CTO of your client, Acme Company, on LinkedIn. This could be a sign that some defensive moves are needed to protect your client relationship.

A simple way to manage the flow of all these conversations is to set up notifications using tools or applications designed for social listening. Google Alerts is free and works well for getting regular email notifications on a company, individual names, or specific topics. You may find more sophisticated enterprise solutions are required, depending on the scope of your social media programs.

Once your monitoring system is set up, you'll need a process to manage the information. It may be as simple as setting aside a few minutes each week to review news and updates. Larger firms with more resources might take a big data approach, sending competitive media mentions to a monitoring team to combine with information from with other sources.

Because patterns that emerge over time can hint at upcoming changes or competitive actions you want to watch—such as new products in development—create a filing system or database to store your alerts and reports. Use keywords or topics to group data points so they can easily be retrieved when you need them.

Consider developing competitive dashboards to track month-to-month metrics for key indicators like hiring or product price changes and promotions. You can pick up on subtle shifts by watching employee posts as well as public data provided by your competitor's PR team or recruiting staff.

Sentiment is another strong leading indicator of competitors that are improving or declining in stature. If your social media monitoring exposes a growing number of negative messages, complaints, or just expressions of frustration, pay attention. These concerns may hint at problems the company would prefer to keep under wraps, like late deliveries due to component shortages or a floundering implementation of new technology.

Understanding your competitors' pain points will help you sell against them in the short term, while informing your competitive strategy for long-term planning. For example, if you see that a company is struggling with employee retention, you might want to step up recruiting to entice top talent you'd like to have on your team. At the same time, you might explore the reasons employees are leaving to get at deeper issues.

Post a Lookout

In medieval times, every castle had a lookout, someone responsible for watching the landscape to see what was coming down the road. Your business needs a lookout, too.

In the modern world, this translates to a system of observations: methods for listening to the market, hearing customer needs, and sensing trends that will impact your business.

Technology provides a wealth of tools to make this possible, from social listening platforms that let you tune in to the online grapevine to CRM systems for monitoring customer interactions.

Data is everywhere.

If you're too busy to analyze it yourself, there are plenty of resources that can help. Industry analysts and associations will keep you abreast of market changes and competitive activities. Even your own sales team and customer service representatives can provide invaluable information about shifts in the business climate.

Use these resources to channel actionable information to your door so even when you're in the midst of fighting fires, you can see beyond the smoke.

Provide regular feedback to your lookouts so they can improve the quality of the information you receive, and continue to fine-tune your course throughout the year.

This level of exploration goes beyond social media. What you learn online can help you focus your offline efforts as well. Take advantage of social media to keep your finger on the pulse of competitors, and you'll discover plenty of useful information to make your own business more competitive.

Courting Customers

Are Your Targeting the Right Customers?

This question digs deeper than general analysis of target markets or who the typical buyers are, focusing instead on the best prospective customers for your business—your *ideal* customer.

An ideal customer is the one who is most likely to buy when you get in front of them because your message resonates so well. Think of the kind of person who starts nodding in approval when your sales team tells their story because it aligns so elegantly with their own issues, concerns, and objectives.

When you find this person, they are ready to sign as soon as you prove you can do the job. Ideal prospects are perfectly aligned with your business model, making everything from sales and service to marketing much easier.

How do you find this mythical creature?

There are a number of ways to develop an ideal customer profile, and they all start with a little research and analysis. Set aside preconceived notions of who you *sell* to, and invest time to really understand who *buys* from you and why.

Explore past deals that have gone well, and find patterns in projects that have gone awry. What can you learn from them?

Here's an example:

Mary sells IP phone systems. She thinks every business in her area with a budget above $15,000 and at least 10 employees is a candidate for her solutions, so she spends all her time prospecting and pitching to anyone who meets that criteria, with a very low close rate.

Frustrated, Mary sits down and reviews her sales activity over the past year, and discovers some patterns. What she finds is this:

- The deals that closed most quickly were ones where Mary met with an educated buyer, who had already done some research on IP vs. traditional phone systems.

- She invested a lot of time with prospects that weren't well informed, educating them about benefits only to be told they weren't ready to make a change, or that they had gone with a competitor.

- Her best buyers were not IT managers or CIOs, but small business owners who understood the bottom line value of the enhanced feature set her phone system offered and how it could impact productivity.

- She also learned that the clients who were most decisive were those that were in growth mode and needed to leverage productivity improvements for improved profitability.

- Finally, she realized that a predefined budget was less important than having an empowered client who:

  1) Understood the value of Mary's services, and
  2) Had the authority to spend what was needed on communications technology.

As a result of this exercise, Mary defined five key criteria for her ideal customers. Then she developed a simple checklist to use as a benchmark for prospects. She began rating every potential customer she met, comparing them to her clearly defined Ideal Client Profile.

Almost immediately, Mary learned that prospects that met four or five of the criteria were worth pursuing because her close rate was much higher. She also discovered that if a prospect scored a 3 on her scale, they had the potential to be a good client, but the path was much longer and the odds of success were lower.

Mary also understood that prospects meeting just one or two of her key filters were not a good match for her business. They might buy eventually. When they did, she would have a hard time fully satisfying their needs and they would be unlikely to provide referrals to other solid prospects.

Using this knowledge, Mary adjusted her sales approach. When she met a prospect that was not a good fit, she referred them to another firm that could better meet their needs. She focused her efforts on finding the four- and five-star prospects, spending less time on meetings and proposals, but closing a much higher percentage of the deals she bid on.

The beauty of this approach is that it can work for any organization that invests the time to define their ideal client.

There are numerous benefits to working with the right customers. For example, it improves satisfaction because you are better able to serve them. Happy customers spread the word, attracting more customers like them. This creates an ongoing pattern of accelerating sales cycles and increasing profitability.

This is especially valuable for any business that depends on referrals or recommendations—and most do these days. With online reviews and the viral nature of business communities, doing business with the right customers has a huge downstream impact on both brand and reputation.

This benefit cycle allows you to continuously raise the bar, moving your business closer to its sweet spot:

- Referral quality improves as your ideal customers introduce you to more companies with similar profiles.

- Working with these buyers enhances customer satisfaction because your business is optimized to serve them well.

- Satisfied customers spread the word, building your brand and attracting more high-quality customers.

Put Your Ideal Customer Profile to Work

Pinpointing your best prospects can dramatically improve sales re-sults and accelerate business growth—if you diligently apply the concept of an ideal customer profile.

Doing so requires work at first. The challenge is that understanding who your best prospects are is one thing, and actually adapting your organization to focus on them is another.

The whole concept can be revolutionary for executives who have al-ways assumed that any business is good business. Developing and using an ideal customer profile will likely also lead to shifts in your own thinking about new business opportunities.

Making the transition is important because time spent with customers outside your target profile takes your company further away from its goals, making success more elusive. By focusing your sales and mar-keting efforts on the prospects with the best potential, you reduce wasted time and effort, alleviating the stress of trying to serve cus-tomers who aren't the right fit.

To avoid being distracted by customers that do not match your ideal client profile, arm your team with a checklist of key customer charac-teristics. Include things like the buyer's knowledge level or business role. Highlight the attitudes that you look for in your best prospects as well. Keep the list short, with five or at most six criteria.

This will make it easier for your team to identify top prospects. Once you understand who they are, develop the discipline to avoid those that don't fit the model, because they cost you money in the long run.

Don't be afraid to say "no"

When applying your ideal customer profile, you will need to say "No, thanks," to opportunities that aren't a good fit. (If you can't bypass the wrong customers, you'll never succeed in courting the right ones.)

This can be difficult for sales people who are measured on number of the number of prospects in their funnel, or those who are expected to have a certain dollar volume in the pipeline at any given time.

It may seem counter-intuitive to walk away from business opportunities. You and your staff might feel frustrated at what feels like leaving money on the table. That is, until you see the power of the profile at work.

Moving to an ideal client profile requires filtering prospects. The sales funnel will be narrower at the top because you're being more selective and not everyone will make the cut. You can expect a much higher close rate from prospects that do enter the funnel, so performance metrics for your sales team may need to be adjusted.

Once the profile becomes part of your regular sales qualification process, closing deals will become easier because you are working with the right contacts from the start. Instead of dealing with endless objections, you'll be illustrating value and sharing successes.

Integrate for impact

To get the biggest impact from your ideal customer profile, integrate it into your operations wherever you can.

Use your ideal client profile to tailor not only your sales process, but also to focus marketing messages and educate your referral sources. In fact, building a profile of your preferred prospects is a great place to start when you are repositioning a business or trying to reinvigorate growth.

Here are four ways to take advantage of these benefits...

1. Train your sales and marketing staff on how to appeal to your best customers through your formal and informal communications. Your sales presentations, collateral and advertising should address hot buttons for your target prospects.

2. Use what author Michael Port calls the "red velvet rope" to filter out prospects who don't fit the mold. If you need highly respon-

sive customers, say so. Provide examples and case studies that highlight the kinds of customers you want to attract.

3. Tailor the way you do business to the needs of your best customers. Test every aspect of your customer experience to be sure it works for them. Incorporate their feedback to improve the quality of your interactions and entice them to not only return, but to tell their friends or colleagues.

4. Exit gracefully from relationships that aren't working well. When a contract is up or a major decision point arises, respectfully part ways. Do customers a favor and connect them with another firm that can better meet their needs, and they'll still appreciate you.

Finally, for the best results, avoid a hit or miss implementation. Stick to your guns and apply the approach consistently to enjoy the full power and impact of laser-focused targeting.

When to Let Go

If you're committed to serving your ideal customers, you must learn to let others go. I know it sounds counterintuitive, but sometimes saying goodbye is the right thing to do.

In fact, there was an interesting case study in the Harvard Business Review about whether a company should fire one of its oldest and "best" customers because they had become a loser in terms of revenue for a couple of quarters.[5]

Unless you're running a charity, the goal is for every customer to yield positive returns. However, sometimes customers do cost more than they spend. When this is the case it can be hard to decide whether to cut your losses or keep the relationship alive.

---

[5] Robert S. Kaplan. *Case Study: When to Drop an Unprofitable Customer.* Harvard Business Review. January 25, 2012. http://blogs.hbr.org/2012/01/case-study-when-to-drop-an-unp/

Knee-jerk decisions to dump a client in the face of a bad quarter, unusually high support costs, or other potentially transitory issues could turn out to be expensive in the long run.

Instead, follow a careful process to assess the true worth of the customer, and then make your decision.

Customer value comes in many forms

We traditionally think of black and white, dollars and cents profit and loss. This seemingly simple measure of customer return on investment (ROI) can be misleading because it does not account for intangibles that can make a customer relationship better or worse in the overall mix.

Even with a tool like activity-based costing, which allocates operational costs to customers relative to order volume, the numbers can be deceiving.

What additional factors should you consider when weighing whether to let a customer go? Here are five items to assess before making this important decision:

1. **Prestige**—What is a big-name client worth in terms of the visibility and prestige the relationship brings to your firm? Putting a number on the value of a marquee customer can be hard, but it's worth considering.

2. **Influence**—How valuable are relationships with the executives of the company in question? Are they industry leaders who influence others? Will damaging those relationships hurt your business in the larger context of your industry?

3. **Advocates**—Is this customer the one who agrees without fail to beta test new offerings? To serve as a referral or provide endorsements and testimonials? These are important contributions to your future business and may be hard to replace.

4. **Early Adopters**—Is this company more innovative than others in your portfolio? Do they always say "yes" to the newest offerings, enabling you to sign other, more reluctant yet lucrative, accounts?

5. **Customer Lifetime Value** —Is there solid, long-term potential or significant upside from future sales? A customer struggling due to a temporary setback might be worth keeping or even helping.

All of these items should be taken into account when assessing who to keep and who to let go. There's no clear scorecard to tell you when to part ways with a customer, but if you take the time to look at the big picture, you'll be in a much better position to make a sound decision.

Make the customer evaluation process as consistent a part of your business as annual employee performance reviews or strategic planning sessions.

Adopting a disciplined approach to evaluating your customer base will enable you to regularly prune underperforming customers that are not strategic assets, creating room to do more for those that are the ideal fit for your business.

Dealing with Dissatisfaction

No matter how carefully you cultivate your customer base, there will be times when a customer is unhappy with the service you provide. Sometimes this is due to a product failure, or it could be the result of miscommunication or unrealistic expectations. How can you get back on track?

Remember to keep things in perspective. This is not a personal issue, and it won't destroy your business. If you are committed to delivering quality products and services, you'll find a way to work it out, or at the very least, move on with minimal damage on both sides.

Part of your strategy should address the kinds of relationships you seek with customers. Is your business transactional, with minimal ongoing dialogue? Or do you need to build long-term relationships for recurring business?

When you are selling low cost products to anyone that will buy them, your attitude towards customers may be significantly different from a business that offers a high touch service. If you have recurring revenue streams from subscriptions services, or you sell regular upgrades and enhancements to your offerings, you will want to build a more collaborative customer community.

Understanding the goal of these relationships will guide your decision making regarding how to handle problems and disputes. In any given situation, you must consider:

- **What is the impact for this individual customer?** For example, is it a minor inconvenience from a broken part that can easily be replaced, or has your customer lost revenue because you didn't deliver on time?

- **What will it take to make it right?** Can you offer a replacement or refund, or do you need to provide some other form of compensation?

- **Is the requested resolution feasible** within the context of your business model?

- **Is there a broader impact**, such as a safety concern, that must also be addressed?

- **If unresolved, will this issue affect your brand and reputation?** High profile problems like safety issues or allegations of improper business practices should be taken seriously.

- **Is the fix worth its cost in terms of time, energy and other resources?** What seems like a reasonable request could potentially result in losses you are not willing to bear. Is the price of saving the customer relationship worth it?

Clear policies avoid disputes

Although a legalistic approach to business can become burdensome quickly, the other, freewheeling extreme is equally problematic. Every business needs to have certain policies and procedures in place to preempt conflicts and complaints.

Creating a basic framework for how you handle routine issues like refunds and returns can avert problems before they occur. Even if your business is still very small, you should plan ahead rather than waiting until issues arise.

Poet Robert Frost says, "Good fences make good neighbors," and I say good policies make good customers (and employees, too). If your business has not paid much attention to policies, choosing to take a reactive stance rather than being proactive, you should reconsider.

Establish a minimum set of policies that includes:

1. How you handle returns and/or refunds.

2. Standard payment terms, methods, and options (including how you handle of past due accounts and interest charges).

3. Terms and conditions of sale, especially if there are limits or restrictions on how your product is used.

4. Copyright restrictions and permissible use for content or materials made accessible to customers.

5. Blog commenting policies.

6. Website terms of use.

7. Guarantees and warrantees, if you have them.

8. Customers or vendors recruiting your employees.

Once you establish your policies, apply them uniformly so employees and customers alike learn what to expect when doing business with you. In certain cases, you may elect to waive a policy, but do so only if there is a sound reason. Otherwise, people may perceive the inconsistency as lack of leadership, favoritism, or worse yet, discrimination.

Invention and Innovation

There is a lot of pressure on growing businesses to continuously innovate in products, services, and even business models. This endless quest for the next big thing leads many executives to rely on customers for creative insights and ideas.

Unfortunately, customers do not have all the answers, especially when it comes to innovation.

Surprised? It's true.

Customers can do a great job of helping you iterate products. They know that, "This button would work better over here," or "That knob always gets in the way." Customers are happy to share new feature requests, like "We'd love it if you could add custom reports to your software," but their insights usually stop right about there.

Customers know how to *improve* your products because they *use* your products. They understand what works, what does not, what makes them crazy, and what is missing. But when it comes to breakthrough solutions, they're often lost.

Think about it. If your customers really knew how to solve their own problems, they wouldn't need you or your solutions. They would go start their own business addressing that need and make loads of money in the process.

You're the Leader

Customers typically have a good understanding of their issues. But they need you to solve them.

How does this subtle difference between iteration and innovation impact your business? If you want to be the runaway leader in your space, it is imperative to move beyond the norm. Stop thinking about different flavors of the same solution, and cook up a different recipe altogether.

One approach is to explore the goal behind the task at hand. What are your customers trying to accomplish? Their objectives may range from something as simple as listening to music to a complex activity like processing a payment.

Sony and Apple both took a radical approach to delivering music to individuals, first with the Walkman and then with the iPod. Not a single customer knew they needed these devices before they entered the market. Customers simply could not envision these solutions to their music listening task.

These two companies are modern examples of radical innovation. Search the annals of history and you'll find a host of similar stories. Did we know we needed the light bulb before Thomas Edison came along? What about cars, TVs, and skateboards? The public was not clamoring for these products, but they sure were happy to buy them when someone else thought them up!

Innovation is not limited to consumer products. Creative solutions to industrial problems can transform manufacturing, production, and delivery of products. Software can change the way people work. Look around and you'll see all kinds of innovation opportunities masked as unsolved—or inadequately solved—problems.

Challenge your team to think differently about these problems and you may find a radically better solution. That innovation may be more elegant, streamlined, and efficient than what you offer today.

Smart Selling

When you started your business, you were most likely the chief cook and bottle washer, and the head of sales and business development, too. Many entrepreneurs are initially successful because they are good sales people—bringing on customers, pitching investors, and selling their vision to anyone who will listen.

Strong sales skills are a great asset to a new business owner, but these same skills can also be a hurdle to growth. If you're not a natural salesperson, you may actually be in a better position to grow your business than someone who is.

Here's why:

For people who excel at sales, handing the reins to someone else can be a difficult. It's hard to relinquish responsibility for something that comes so easy and means so much. If you've been in this position, you know how tempting it is to stick your nose into every deal and constantly ride herd over your reps. It can be hard to step back and let them do their jobs.

Learning to let go of the sales process can be one of the most important things you do for you business. After all, if you want focus on leading your business, it is hard to sell, too.

Awesome sales people have a tendency to look for replication of their personal sales model when hiring sales staff. They want someone to "do it the way I do." That will probably never happen. No matter how good you are, you can't be cloned.

In order to build a repeatable sales model, think about what you do well and why it works. Document your approach, tools and processes, and train you sales team on how to use these resources.

Do not expect an exact duplicate of your efforts. Each rep will adapt your process to their own personality and work style, developing a method that is comfortable for them. That's OK. In fact, you may discover that your team refines your model and delivers improvements you never would have conceived.

When you hold your regular sales meetings, get beyond the quota discussion to share case studies of both successes and failures. Don't be judgmental. Listen and learn, then adapt your formal process and tools to reflect the evolution of your approach.

Are You Using the Right Sales Model?

Many businesses use a direct sales model, putting "feet on the street" to call on prospects. Building personal connections through face-to-face contact is important for some businesses. It is also the most expensive way to sell your products and services. Depending on the nature of your business, you may be able to increase profitability by choosing a different approach.

Picking a sales model that works

You have many options for selling, from direct sales with a team of field sales representatives to inside sales, calls centers, or online sales that are 100% self-service. The best choice for you will depend greatly on your customers' needs and how they prefer to purchase products, as well as the relative cost and efficiency of each channel.

Some questions to consider when selecting a sales channel include:

How complex is your offering? Does it require a great deal of explanation or configuration? If it is a simple, out of the box product or application, you do not need a team of reps selling it face-to-face. Online or catalog sales may suffice.

How long is your sales cycle? Do you need to provide extensive customer education over a period of weeks or months before a prospect becomes a customer? If so, having a dedicated sales representative, and even a support team to assist with training and education, can be an advantage.

Content marketing, videos, webinars and other resources can aid in the education process. With B2B customers completing nearly 60% of a typical decision cycle before even having a conversation with a supplier, these tools are becoming increasingly vital to success in complex sales.[6]

Is your product pricey or inexpensive? Purchasers of low-cost offerings do not require nearly as much handholding as those buying luxury goods or complex products. In this case, it is not just about educating buyers, it's about trust and relationships, too.

Someone shelling out big bucks for a product needs to be treated like a highly valued customer so they walk away feeling good about the buying experience.

Are you dealing in high volume? Buyers of high volume goods, such as those needed for industrial applications will expect to have access to a sales person who is educated about their needs.

The sales representative may be expected to spend time on-site with the customer, who may even participate in discussions of product requirements to help influence your product roadmap.

Is customization important? Depending on the type of customization required, you may find an online or mobile solution can help buyers configure products and place orders with minimal sales interaction.

---

[6]Ana Lapter. 2011. *The Most Important Number in B2B Marketing*. CEB Marketing. http://www.executiveboard.com/marketing-blog/the-most-important-number-in-b2b-marketing/ (accessed Mach 20, 2014).

On the other hand, some customization decisions require assistance from someone who can advise a buyer on the best options for their needs. This can be done in person, via web chat or over the phone.

Is your product a commodity? If you are selling a product that can be purchased from a number of vendors, like office supplies or packaged software, your customers are much more likely to be shopping based on price and service (quick delivery or free shipping, for example).

In this case, Internet and telesales are good options because they are more cost effective than retail stores or direct sales.

Do customers need to see, touch, and feel your product? Buyers of items like fabric, kitchen cabinets, or granite want to get up close with your product before making a purchase. A store or showroom can address this need.

Providing easy access to samples requested through a website and delivered directly to a customer can also work. In fact, this is how I bought carpet for my basement, and it turned out beautifully.

Sale channel options

Table 6 shows a number of sales channels and how they are commonly utilized. These are typical, not mandatory, applications. Some businesses have found a great degree of success by thwarting conventional wisdom about the accepted way to sell a given type of product, developing a competitive advantage by using an alternate channel.

The online shoe store Zappos is a perfect example of this. Before they started selling shoes on the Internet, it was rarely done by anyone but established catalog sales companies that transitioned to an online model.

It was assumed that no one would buy shoes online because fit was such a strong consideration in the purchase process. By removing this issue with a liberal return policy, Zappos successfully created an online sales model that is dramatically more cost effective than brick and mortar stores.

Feel free to think unconventionally when deciding on your sales model. Be ready to adjust other areas of your strategy and operations to ensure that all systems work in concert. Marketing distribution, delivery, and customer service must all be coordinated for optimal results.

Table 6: Sales Channels

Sales Channel	Best for...
Online (Internet) Sales	A wide variety of products and services, including stock items and highly customized products.
Inside Sales Reps (inbound or outbound call centers)	Standard items or those that can be easily customized. Products and services that require minimal explanation.
Retail Storefront	Consumer products, both mass market and boutique offerings.
Outside Sales / Field Sales Reps	B2B products and services, especially those with long sales cycles or complex configuration.
Resellers / Distributors	Access to hard-to-penetrate markets and wide distribution.
Third-Party Reps / Manufacturers Reps	Wholesale, B2B or industrial sales.
Omni-Channel	Combines multiple channels, usually web, phone and stores, providing a unified experience.

Shifting your model

Selecting the right sales model is a strategic decision that will have lasting implications for your business. However, if you realize that making a change will increase revenues or profitability, by all means, make the transition.

To avoid upsetting customers, shift gradually by ramping up the new approach (say, telesales teams) and winding down the old one (field sales reps, for example), allowing for a period of overlap or parallel operations during which customers can adapt to the new approach.

Communicate regularly with customers before, during, and after the change. Let them know why you are modifying your approach and clearly explain how it benefits them. If your new sales model gives customers better access to sales support, faster response to inquiries or lower prices as a reflection of your reduced costs, say so.

Sales and Marketing Alignment

Who's Lead Is It, Anyway?

If you're looking for a topic where Sales and Marketing disagree, lead generation is a hot one. Listen in on any conversation between the two departments and you're likely to hear something like this:

> **Marketing**: "Why don't you ever follow up on the leads we send you?"

> **Sales**: "Because the leads you give us stink!"

The conversation can quickly decay into a debate over what exactly *is* a lead, or even a shouting match on the merits of lead generation and the perceived arrogance of marketing or the laziness of sales people.

Don't go there!

Before the relationship between your Sales and Marketing teams deteriorates to that degree—and especially if it has already—you need some clarity around lead generation.

Where's the Disconnect?

The friction over leads is not uncommon and the reason is simple: Sales and Marketing are each approaching lead generation from a different angle, with different priorities:

- Marketing needs to connect with as many viable prospects as possible. They're in the business of generating lead volume.

- Sales must be as efficient as possible. To avoid wasting time with unqualified prospects, their focus is on lead quality.

Sales wants hot prospects while Marketing is content with a simple inquiry. That inquiry may represent a warm lead to Marketing, but it is not a real lead, at least not to Sales.

For Sales, a real lead is a qualified contact that has expressed an active interest in purchasing something you offer in the near future.

For Marketing, a lead is someone who has expressed a vague interest, or who is assumed to have an interest, in what you sell, without any definite time frame attached.

The difference? For Sales, leads are **immediately actionable contacts**, ripe fruit ready to be picked. For Marketing, leads include this sweet fruit, as well as **seeds to be nurtured** for future harvests.

Some Sales teams, especially in B2B organizations with a long sales cycle, begin to plan the harvest as soon as the fruit starts to develop. In other words, any prospect that is being actively courted goes into the sales funnel for tracking.

In other organizations, Sales waits for the signal that it is picking time. They hold off on moving prospects into the funnel until there are serious discussions taking place.

Either way, the organizations that are the most effective at closing leads are diligent in coordinating the handoff from Marketing to Sales. They plan the right time for the transition so that Marketing has effectively cultivated the contact and Sales can harvest the deal.

A Better Approach

If you want your sales and marketing efforts to be successful start by defining what, exactly, *is* a lead in terms that both Sales and Marketing can agree upon.

Define terms that can be shared throughout your organization to express where a lead is along the sales cycle. For example, you may move from "contacts" to "inquiries" to "qualified leads" to "prospects" to "proposals."

Many organizations also create a separate class of marketing leads that I like to call "nurture" leads. These are the people who may have a future interest, but aren't ready to buy. These leads should not be discarded, but they certainly do not belong in the sales funnel yet.

Marketing is the ideal place to foster leads using a predictable, proven series of touch points. These educated and informed leads result in shorter sales cycles. When leads mature into qualified prospects they can be closed quickly, making Sales and management happy.

A shared understanding of the various types of leads, the stages of the sales cycle, and who owns leads in each phase replaces conflict with collaboration and improves your bottom line.

Chapter 6

Customer Experience

Do Your Customers Really Come First?

How often do you make a call to a business, only to hear the frustrating refrain, *"Your call is important to us…"*

Really?

No matter how often companies say their customers come first, the reality is often somewhat different. We know intuitively that customers count. They pay the bills, after all. But so often, other priorities creep up, pushing the customer further and further down the line.

Here are a few examples, including some from my own experiences:

Not So Rewarding

To help with my office supply expenses, I joined the Staples Rewards loyalty program for discounts and special offers. Soon after, a promotional email for copier paper caught my eye. Staples included a coupon for an extra $5 off a case of paper purchased in the store rather than online. The advertised sale price of $24.99 was a great deal to begin with, and stopping by on my weekly round of errands to save an extra $5 seemed worth the trouble.

At the register I learned that the price advertised was the net amount after an "Easy Rebate." By "easy," Staples meant I could fill out some paperwork and wait for them to mail me a Visa gift card. If I wanted to buy the paper outright, the real price at the register was $49.99. (Yes, you read that right, double the advertised price!)

Needless to say, I left without the paper.

Instead of building my loyalty, Staples destroyed what little it had. My perception was that my only "reward" was the privilege of being misled. Staples didn't want to reward me at all. They simply wanted to sell more office supplies.

Missing Miles

An article in The Wall Street Journal[7] reported on musicians flying with cellos—a rather large instrument—having to buy extra seats for their instruments. According to the article, some passengers had been encouraged to open Delta SkyMiles accounts for these companion instruments, only to be informed later that this was against Delta's policies.

One unfortunate musician, Lynn Harrell, lost the miles in both his account and that of his cello. A Delta spokesperson was quoted as saying, "An object doesn't have a loyalty experience." An object doesn't buy airline tickets, either, but that doesn't stop Delta from selling the ticket.

The problem is that Delta (like all airlines with frequent flyer programs) doesn't really offer incentive miles to acknowledge customer loyalty. These so-called "loyalty programs" are designed to encourage people to fly Delta more often, not to reward past behavior.

The fact that these programs are profit-driven, not customer-centered, is underscored by major changes in the Delta SkyMiles program, which will reward higher spending rather than actual miles flown.[8]

---

[7] Scott McCartney. *When Flying, Are Cellos People Too?* Wall Street Journal. March 13, 2013.

[8] Charisse Jones. *Delta Frequent-Flier Plan Now Tied to Airfare.* USAToday. February 27, 2014

Limited Support

When updating apps on my iPad, I noticed that one update required the latest operating system from Apple. Although my iPad showed I had the latest software, the version number didn't seem current so I did a little digging. Come to find out, my aging iPad (not even two years old) could not get the latest operating system software from Apple because that version of the iPad was no longer supported.

This happens all the time with technology products, so I wasn't terribly surprised. However, my Google search on the topic uncovered many irritated customers, several with iPads they had only owned for 18 months or so that could no longer be updated. If I had paid nearly $800 for my iPad, I would have been unhappy, too. Thankfully, I got a deal on a refurbished one, so the pain was slightly less intense.

As passionate Apple customers, people posting online were outraged that Apple was putting more emphasis on new product releases than on their customers' need for products with a long functional life.

Overcoming Ambivalence

If any of these scenarios strike a chord of familiarity with you, then you know how it feels to encounter the "We love our customers...sort of," attitude of many businesses.

You might even recognize similarities here with your own company's business practices. Perhaps you're thinking, "We'd go broke if we did everything the customer wanted." I'm not suggesting that you do, but let me challenge that position for a moment.

Executives learn in business school that the objective of a company is to generate revenue—or financial returns—for owners and shareholders. I'll hazard a guess that why you're in business, too. After all, if you're not making money, what's the point, right?

Here's a different point of view:

Businesses exist to serve customers first, not to make money.

I know that sounds like heresy, but income is a *by-product* of effectively meeting customer needs. When organizations lose sight of the fact that customers are the most critical ingredients for business success, you get policies and processes that are more focused on profit, efficiency, and employee convenience than on serving customers.

This can work for a while—months, sometimes even years—but in the end it leads to a downward spiral. Customers love to hate businesses like these. They leave as soon as a viable alternative becomes available, and business falters.

Before this happens to your company, ask yourself, "What happens when we put customers first?"

When you focus on meeting the needs of the right customers (because you can't serve everyone), you'll discover that they share their experience with others, and they want to repeat it again and again. They become truly loyal rather than artificially so.

These customers are more profitable than those that feel no choice but to do business with a company. Turning the cycle around and putting customers at the forefront of business decisions makes an indelible imprint on an organization. Happy customers create profits and fuel growth.

Cultivating Customer Experience

Beyond the Front Line

Intuitively, it's easy to understand how customer-facing employees make a difference in your buyer's experience, but profitable relationships go much deeper than the front line. They depend on everyone in your organization and reflect the underlying culture that shapes your brand.

The connection between brand and culture is important, and we'll dig deep into the brand side of the equation in Chapter 7. For now, let's focus on the customer component.

When your brand resonates with customers, it shows that your business strategy is in tune with customer needs. If there is a disconnect, customers won't believe your brand messages because they are either not customer-centric, or your employees and policies are undermining them.

Much as a parent may say, "Do as I say, not as I do," we know that actions speak louder than words. You have to send you customers the right message by carefully aligning your strategy, brand, and customer experience to create momentum in your business.

It's not just a touchy-feely thing

Some numbers-driven executives may dismiss culture as the "feel good" domain of HR professionals, but that's a big mistake. It's not just about the warm and fuzzies.

Even twenty years ago, studies showed the powerful connection between company culture and improved business performance.[9] In 1992, Harvard professors John Kotter and James Heskett compared the performance of 200 organizations that made company culture a key aspect of their strategy and those that did not.

The difference was dramatic, showing that:

- Revenues increased four times faster,
- Job creation rates were seven times higher,
- Profits were 750% higher, and
- Customer satisfaction doubled.

Can you create results like that?

It is possible. Recently, we've seen a number of examples where companies that focused on culture have delivered outstanding results.

---

[9] John P. Kotter and James Heskett. *Corporate Culture and Performance.* New York: Simon & Schuster, 1992.

The Gem Shopping Network tripled its revenues in two years by listening to employees, understanding their challenges and addressing them.[10]

This included providing employees with additional education and tools to make their job easier. It also involved executives becoming more present and visible in the business, so that employees could see they were willing to work just as hard as their staff.

The telecom company Grasshopper is another example.[11] The founders were struggling to grow from about $10M in annual revenue to their goal or $20 million or more. They wisely realized there were some items holding them back.

One was lack of a clear culture, so they invested in leadership assessments for the senior team and spent time clarifying the core values they wanted the company to embody. This enabled them to be more focused in both expressing their culture and in hiring employees that were a cultural fit.

As a result, their turnover decreased from 25% to just 10% while market share increased and operational results improved.

Connecting Culture to Customer Relationships

The fact is that whether it's healthy or not, your corporate culture is reflected in the way employees interact with customers, suppliers, and partners.

Exceptional leaders understand that culture is crafted from the top down, and it's a key indicator of the health and welfare of your corporate vision. Corporate culture is also a critical component of customer relationships that last.

Here are five ways your corporate culture influences business success:

---

[10] H.M. Cauley. *Golden Opportunity: CEO changes corporate culture to boost revenue at Gem Shopping Network Inc.* Atlanta Business Chronicle. September 20, 2013.

[11] Amy S. Choi. *To Boost Efficiency, Rethink Company Culture.* Entrepreneur. April 17, 2013.

1. Caring or callous?

Employees who care treat customers well, employees who don't, won't. Some people naturally have a more caring and compassionate nature, but caring can be instilled in your culture as well. Do managers and executives know people by name? Do they take time to ask about interests, hobbies, and family? If so, is this interest sincere or a simple formality?

If you've ever worked for a boss who could barely remember your name, you know that's not a good environment!

Showing care and concern for others, both personally and professionally, makes a difference. When a caring attitude is part of everyday work life, it quickly extends into customer interactions with a similar approach.

2. Ethics are contagious

If you want employees to deal ethically with customers and suppliers, start by modeling appropriate behavior within your firm. Little lies or half-truths from leaders suggest that it's ok to stretch the truth. Once people cross that line, it's hard to remember where the boundary was in the first place.

Things like fudging on expenses (picture the supervisor who says to employees, "Don't worry, I can write this off," when he shouldn't), pilfering supplies for personal use or intentionally undermining co-workers may seem like minor infractions, but people notice.

Employees get the unwritten message and before you know it, customer relationships begin to suffer from the suspicion and lack of trust that flows downstream.

The "I'll get mine and I don't care what it costs you," attitude becomes prevalent, seeping into customer interactions as well as inter-office relationships.

3. Going the extra mile

When going above and beyond is recognized and rewarded within the company, employees are more likely to do what it takes to meet customer needs. Do managers go out of their way to communicate effectively with employees? Do they work hard to solicit feedback and act on concerns?

If shoddy work is routinely accepted, when people drop the ball on projects without consequences, these habits will extend to interactions with customers. Emphasize follow-through, attention to detail, and a "make it happen" approach internally and enjoy the same level of accountability when dealing with customers.

The Publix grocery store chain excels at this. If you're in a store and you need to find something, any employee you ask will personally escort you to the location to be sure you find the item. Publix also looks after its employees, offering stock and scholarships opportunities to everyone from baggers to senior management. The result is a marked difference in experience compared with other grocery store chains.

4. Empowered for action

When employees know they have the latitude to act on issues without fear of micromanagement or retribution for coloring outside the lines, they also feel empowered to creatively address customer concerns.

Creating a framework within which employees have the flexibility to make decisions is empowering. It shows trust for employees and encourages actions that support co-workers as well as customers. Let employees demonstrate that they have the ability and desire to make things happen, and customer loyalty skyrockets.

5. Do the right thing

When you treat your employees well, insisting on professionalism, respect, and consideration, it shows inside and out. Like creating an environment of trust, mutual respect and the commitment to "do the right thing" increases employee commitment.

Employees who know that they will be treated fairly even when the news isn't good will extend the same courtesy to customers. Instead of placing blame or shirking responsibility, companies that value integrity emphasize honesty, candid comments, and making it right.

Ritz Carlton is famous for this. Their motto is *"We are Ladies and Gentlemen serving Ladies and Gentlemen."* That philosophy shapes everything they do, and it exemplifies the attitude that "the genuine care and comfort of our guests is our highest mission."[12]

How's Your Business Doing?

Do you recognize your business in any of these scenarios? Do you have teams or departments that serve as models for good or bad performance in these areas?

Watch for these four trouble indicators as early warning signs:

- High employee turnover
- Poor customer retention or declining repeat business
- Slowing momentum or growth
- An epidemic of missed goals or commitments

If you think your culture is inhibiting business growth, assess the magnitude and type of problem you're facing. It could be minor or more significant and knowing if you're dealing with a mouse or an elephant is important.

Use these three methods to quickly identify the nature and scope of the issue:

First, get the customer's point of view. Talk with customers, review comments and feedback, or listen in on sales and support calls. What is being said (or not said) that indicates were the problems are?

---

[12] Ritz Carlton. *Gold Standards.*
http://corporate.ritzcarlton.com/en/About/GoldStandards.htm (accessed March 6, 2014).

Is there a stark contrast between good interactions and less positive ones? Make notes about what works and what doesn't, they will come in handy later.

Next, look at employee interactions. Are there major silos or conflicts within the organization? Do employees badmouth each other, disparage different departments, or place blame?

Discord can be a real issue following an acquisition if the firms were fierce competitors prior to the merger. It can also appear when managers don't get along and pit their teams against each other.

This particular issue may be hard to pinpoint as an executive because employees can be reluctant to tell you the truth about what's going on. If that's the case, this is a good time to employ a secret shopper or a consultant who can shadow employees or interview them to get objective feedback.

Finally, check for fluid information transfer. Are the only messages effectively disseminated coming from the rumor mill? Are there disagreements or misunderstandings on fundamental things like strategic direction or key policies?

Failure to share information and refusal to buy into company initiatives are signs that trust and communication have broken down.

Once you have a handle on where you stand, start exploring possible solutions. These should be holistic, and not simply Band-Aids to mask a problem. Address the root cause, whether it is overworked employees, conflicting policies, poor training, or problems with management.

The right solutions will be unique to your business, but you can take cues from companies that have succeeded. Spend some time exploring organizations that are doing well and see how they are different from your business. What can you learn from them?

Another success factor is that your commitment to developing a customer-friendly culture needs to be long term and not what I call the "flavor of the month." Your efforts should become ingrained in your business, rolled into the culture as intentionally as the changes you make.

Ideally, your efforts will begin with customer needs. That's different that trying to please everyone. Focus on your market and your ideal customers. Ask, "How can we better serve our customers?" and you'll be headed in the right direction.

Other cultural consideration, like being persistently budget conscious, relentlessly pursuing innovation, or being extremely operationally efficient, should be addressed within the context of customer relationships.

Ask your team how you can do these things in the service of your customers. Objectives like innovation and efficiency are rarely ends in themselves. Instead, they make it possible for you to offer lower prices, create new products, or provide more efficient delivery.

Be transparent in your communications with your employees about the changes you decide to make. You don't need to say, "We've concluded it is time for a new culture." That might backfire.

Let you people know why the changes are happening in relation to your corporate strategy and objectives. Sharing core values like, "We put customers first" or "Every employee owns our success," can provide context for change.

Create an environment where the changes you need make perfect sense to employees, and even serve their self-interest. They'll be more motivated to embrace them than if you take an authoritative, "my way or the highway," approach.

Once underway, go back periodically to check your progress relative to the three assessment methods I provided at the start of this section. Are things improving? If not, why not? Maybe there is an unintended consequence at work, or resistance from a key employee that needs to be addressed.

Stick with it. As your efforts take hold, you'll begin to see benefits in the bottom line with reduced employee and customer turnover and improved satisfaction on all fronts.

Beyond Customer Delight

If you're at all concerned with customer experience, I'm sure you've heard (or read) about "delighting the customer." This concept is bounced around as if it's the panacea for all corporate ills.

Simply delight your customers, and business will be booming, right? Not so fast: Do you really need to delight your customers?

Based on my years of work in customer loyalty and retention, and my experience helping companies connect their corporate vision with customer reality, I have to challenge the assumption that delight is a goal we should all be pursuing.

Of course, delighting customers sounds good on the surface. Who wouldn't want customers to express delight about the quality of service provided or the exceptional value delivered by their products?

Delight is a good thing, right?

Creating experiences that delight our customers is not inherently wrong. However, making "delight" the aim of all aspects of customer engagement is simply the wrong goal for most companies.

What Is Delight?

Think about it. When you're really delighted, how do you feel? Are you euphoric? Giddy? Surprised?

Picture a six-year old skipping around the yard upon receiving their first bike or a newly engaged couple. How about the proud pet parents with a new puppy? That's delight.

Delight is a transitory emotion, brought on by an often unexpected, yet positive, turn of events.

It is a feeling of extreme satisfaction, a high degree of gratification.

That's precisely where the problem is. Delight is an emotional high that is difficult to sustain, one that would lose its potency if it were to become a constant state.

When delight becomes the norm, the impact of the experience wanes, making the next high harder and harder to achieve.

Instead of constantly aiming to create an ethereal delight experience, I advise pursuing more enduring goals. Whether the emotion you seek to inspire is called satisfaction or gratification or simply pleasure is less important than the fact the experience you create is both sustainable and memorable for customers.

Delight Fades, Experience Endures

An optimal customer experience goes beyond delight to reinforce the brand value and validate a buyer's purchase decision. It must continue to connect the value of a product or service to the positive emotions associated with the experience long after the purchase transaction is complete.

To create a lasting relationship, your customer experience must etch brand affinity into the hearts and minds of your buyers.

Knowing this, how can you create "memorable moments" that stay with customers longer than delight lasts?

SCORE with Customers

There are a number of factors that shape a highly desirable customer experience. My **SCORE** model illustrates five dimensions of a customer relationship that adds value for both the customer and the corporation.

"SCORE" stands for Sincere, **C**onsistent, **O**rganic, **R**elevant, and **E**nduring interactions. We'll break down each of these dimensions in detail, exploring what they mean and how you can apply the concept in your business.

Sincere

Sincere customer interactions are not scripted. They are not delivered with rote memorization in a cold and unfeeling way.

Although templates and models can be useful for training purposes, employees must internalize the corporate attitude towards customers and express it in a personal way. Then, and only then, are they able to deliver the ideal customer experience with sincerity and authenticity.

We've all had business encounters where the staffers seem to be going through the motions because they've delivered the same spiel so many times. Air travel is one example that readily comes to mind.

Think about the flight attendants running through their safety routine or walking up and down the aisles during the flight repeating the same thing over and over again...

"Pretzels or peanuts?"

"Please bring your seatback up in preparation for landing..."

"Thank you for flying with us."

It's not uncommon for phrases that are repeated again and again to become robotic and lose all meaning. The response, if required, hardly even matters. It's simply part of the routine that comes with the job.

How often do people in service businesses say, "Have a good day" with a scowl on their face, or without even looking at you? What is sincere, the words or the expression? My mother always said, "Actions speak louder than words," and she was right.

While as frustrating as these types of interactions can be, if you fly much, maybe you can recall a few good experiences as well. Remember those times when the flight attendant took the time to speak to you on a personal level? It probably made a huge difference in your flight experience and quite possibly, your whole day. When the person behind the protocol breaks through, you've discovered a sincere interaction.

Consistent

The second element in the SCORE model is *Consistent*. This is different than the example I just gave of how too much consistency can kill the customer experience. That is not what I'm talking about when I refer to consistency as a best practice.

Consistency in this case means that the experience of a customer is coherent at every touch point, before, during and after the sale.

Instead of a cookie-cutter, one-size-fits-all approach to customer interactions, there is congruency across channels and departments in things like the tone of your communications, your brand messaging, the level of access you provide for customers, services and support policies and the like.

This may be one of the most difficult elements to achieve because of the human factors involved. The person you deal with in Sales is not the same person you speak with when you have a problem, and often in larger firms, different departments have varying policies, procedures, and objectives.

Say for example, you go into a company-owned mattress showroom to get a new mattress. Unless the store is super busy, the sales rep is almost certainly going to spend as much time as necessary to make the sale. He won't give you the brush-off or look at his watch as if he can only spare five minutes before his supervisor writes him up for taking too long.

Then what happens *after* you buy the mattress? Let's say you have it delivered and discover a tear in the cover as you're putting on the sheets. You call the customer service number and what happens?

Most likely, after waiting on hold for 10 or 15 minutes, you are finally connected with someone in a call center (which may be outsourced or even off-shore) who starts reading a script, asking a standard list of questions that don't even apply to your situation.

They rush you off the phone so they can meet their arbitrary targets for talk time, and don't seem to care if you felt good about the interaction or not.

That is hardly a pleasant experience, and usually the person you spoke with is not to blame. They are just doing their job.

The underlying problem is that the customer engagement process is broken. That company doesn't have a consistent approach to customer interactions.

Naturally, you didn't change—you're the same person on both sides of the transaction—before and after the sale. But the company's perspective shifted, and that broke the continuity of the relationship. The mattress firm's view of you morphed from a source of potential revenue to a cost to be managed, not an opportunity to win repeat business.

By taking a holistic view of the customer and building this into your business processes, you can ensure that all customer interactions support the same goal: to ensure your customers want to continue to do business with you.

Aligning all of your customer interactions with your corporate philosophies reinforces your brand and creates ongoing value for buyers.

Organic

As you've seen, aligning interactions so they are consistent, but not overly constrained, is important to building enduring relationships.

How do you achieve this?

The key to authentic interactions at all levels of the organization is to understand the organic nature of the customer experience.

There are two aspects of organic experience:

1. Having natural interactions that aren't scripted.
2. The natural flow of internal (employee) experiences to the outside (customers).

The qualities and characteristics of your company's customer experience emanate from deep within the organization, and it's hard to hide the truth if your organization is not customer friendly.

This is because these interactions are by nature an expression of internal attitudes about how customers should be treated.

- Some companies view customers as a necessary evil.

- Some look at them as objects and not people.

- Some only care about the money and not where it comes from.

This attitude typically comes from the top, but even when you have the most customer-focused executive team, things can go awry on the way to the front lines.

In the previous example, the mattress company's policy of measuring customer service reps on the time spent on each call created an incentive that runs counter to customer satisfaction. Maybe the goal of this policy is to ensure more calls can be handled each day, or to reduce wait times, or to do more with fewer people. None of these goals is customer centric.

Understanding the down-stream impact of decisions like these can help avoid the negative impact on customers that erodes your brand reputation and value.

Another aspect of the organic nature of customer relations is the opportunity to empower employees, especially when you're sure they understand the overarching philosophy of your business.

You can do this by hiring for certain customer-orientation traits like the online shoe company Zappos does.[13] In fact, you may have heard that they even offer new hires a bonus to leave after their training period, because the company believes that anyone who is not committed enough to stay shouldn't be there anyway. That may seem extreme, but it works for Zappos.

---

[13] Read *Delivering Happiness: A Path to Profits, Passion, and Purpose* by Zappos' CEO Tony Hsieh for his unconventional perspectives on building a team.

If you're not sure where to start with assessing your firm's natural approach to customers—and by that I mean the organic end result of all your attitudes and policies, start by asking your employees what they think. From the bottom to the top, employees can usually articulate what's distinctive about the way their company interacts with customers, whether it's good or bad.

A big difference of opinion from one level to the next is a sign that what your executive team wants to cultivate in terms of relationships is not what really happens. It's time to dig deeper and find out why.

Relevant

Once you have a handle on the internal or organic aspects of your customer relationships, it's time to start thinking about how your efforts are received.

Relevant customer experiences acknowledge that the best approach to customers is not a one-sided, take-it-or-leave-it attitude. Of course, you can dig your heels in and decide that all policies are non-negotiable, but unless that decision is motivated by safety concerns or regulatory requirements, it likely won't play well with customers.

Relevance considers customer needs and desires, creating experiences that are unique to each customer's needs. Relevant customer interactions are flexible, tailored to the moment and the medium.

You can't standardize relevance, although I'm sure some of us would like to! It's hard to create policies and procedures that ensure that every interaction will appeal to a customer, but there are things you can do the increase the likelihood of meeting a wide variety of needs.

Amazon was a pioneer in creating online relevance with its recommendation engine to match products a customer might want based on purchase behavior or what other people with similar searches bought.

Using data to predict customer needs and preferences can be a wonderful opportunity, but it can also backfire if the data doesn't match up properly.

Suppose, for example, a husband and wife share an account on Amazon.com. One day the wife is shopping for Spanx® shapewear so she can look good in her new dress. Later in the day, the husband logs on to look for something entirely different. He's probably not going to be thrilled to be presented with recommendations for women's shapewear.

An excellent way to create relevance is to train front-line employees on boundary conditions, allowing them to make decisions within the context of certain guidelines.

Ritz Carlton used to give employees a certain spending limit for meeting customer needs. Within that budget of, say $25 per guest, they were able to do things like buy flowers, comp drinks, or deliver a favorite board game to ensure their guests were happy.

When employees don't fear a backlash from making autonomous decisions, they are much more inclined to put the customer's best interests first. They know the organization wants them to put the customer first because it has created an environment in which this is both easy and expected. The culture encourages customer connections, and employees deliver.

This customer-first approach can apply to call center employees, field sales and support staff, or anyone in a position to solve a customer problem.

Beyond problem solving

Relevance doesn't apply just to problem solving. It can also be used as a tool to customize interactions, either on an individual or a segment basis.

Let's suppose you have a local business that deals with families and there are a lot of graduating seniors every spring. Maybe your normal business development efforts involve offering a percent-off discount on services at certain times of the year.

That's nice as a promotion, but what if you offered customers an option of how to use it? How about a choice between a discount at the time of purchase *or* putting the savings on a gift card for the graduating senior? You could even create a fund for regular customers, so that each purchase between January and May accrues funds towards a larger reward to be redeemed at the end of the school year.

Choice increases relevance. People like to have options and control because they can tailor their choices to their own preferences.

Programmatic tailoring of rewards and incentives to targeted groups can be very helpful from a marketing perspective, but the most powerful form of relevance comes from one-on-one connections between employees and customers.

These personal connections enable a real-time, interactive approach to meeting customer needs in the moment. Sometimes, these interactions lead to long-term relationships, like having a personal contact at your bank or an insurance agent who proactively addresses your family's changing needs.

At the same time, relevant interactions can happen any time someone on your team has empathy for a customer's situation and the ability to tailor a solution to accommodate their individual needs.

Enduring

Customers often become passionate about brands, in either a positive and negative way. These feelings run deep and can therefore be extremely hard to unravel if things don't go well from the start.

I'm sure if you take just a moment, you can think of a few brands or companies you have vowed to never buy from again. In contrast, there are probably other businesses you would go miles out of your way to patronize.

Just thinking about these two extremes may inspire a range of deep-seated, emotional reactions. In the SCORE model, we're focused on creating enduring *positive* relationships and helping you avoid negative impressions.

Customer experiences can be highly personal and intensely emotional, even in business-to-business environments. In fact, this is where the whole concept of customer delight comes from. It's an emotional response.

As we've seen, delight is transitory. It's nice to enjoy a free slice of cake after dinner, fresh flowers in your hotel room, or a year's worth of software upgrades at no change. These gifts all buy happiness for a little while. Unfortunately, the feeling is not enduring.

The same has been shown to be true of things like pay increases for employees. The effect wears off after a few short weeks and you're right back where you started.

Creating a workplace that values employees, offers relevant benefits and encourages an attitude of mutual respect is much more likely to entice employees to stay with you and do good work.

Customer relationships follow a similar pattern. Personal interactions fostered by a commitment to relevance have an enduring impact.

Because these interactions go well beyond the transient joy of getting free stuff, they result in more lasting impressions. Reach into customers' emotional core by showing them they are valued and respected, creating both an ongoing relationship and a memorable experience.

Customers who feel connected to your business will often recommend it to others, and they'll come back again and again. Successful companies deliver not only moments of delight, but also enduring satisfaction and memorable interactions.

Fond recollections of mutually beneficial relationships contribute to:

- Customer loyalty

- Repurchase behavior

- Positive word of mouth

- Consistent referrals

Together, these items build brand equity and ultimately add value to the bottom line.

Using the **SCORE** model as a foundation, you can craft customer experiences that leave an indelible, positive imprint on the minds of your customers.

Instead of focusing on pleasing customers in a fleeting moment that will soon be forgotten, equip everyone in your organization to SCORE a lasting impression. The benefits include long-term, loyal customer relationships, increased market share, and accelerated business growth.

Living Value: Brand Meets Customer Experience

In one of my past positions, I worked on speech-recognition applications, finding ways to efficiently handle customer requests with automated solutions. This is a tall order because automated voice response (AVR) technology can easily complicate, not simplify, interactions if the technology is not applied correctly. (*You know what I mean if you've ever tried to get an "Operator" without success.*)

This experience impressed upon me how important it is for organizations to extend their brand to the customer experience, rather than allowing touch points like call centers or self-service solutions to stand on their own.

When I say this, I am not talking about adding advertisements to the recordings you play on hold. I'm not encouraging you to ask every third customer to "please hold to take our survey" so you can find out what they think. What I do mean is that your brand should inform the very architecture of your approach to serving customers.

Instead of simply saying that you want every customer to have a "good" experience when they engage with your company, think about what it really means to deliver service that is consistent with your brand.

- Do customers get stuck in "voice mail jail," running through endless prompts in an effort to get questions answered...while your system is telling them how valuable they are?

- Do you provide live operators with questionable language skills...while touting your "best in class" service?

- Are some agents dramatically more skilled than others at meeting customer needs...creating an inconsistent experience?

Perhaps your efforts to control costs result in unintended consequences for customers. Do you allocate a certain amount of time for an agent to handle each call, causing them to be abrupt instead of taking time to listen to what customers have to say? Are the hours for customer support limited and inconvenient for your target market?

All of these questions are important to ask on a regular basis. The answers will provide clarity in terms of what it's like to be a customer of your company. But they won't specifically indicate that your customer experience is consistent with your brand. For that, you need to dig a little deeper.

Think about the brand messages you project that imply a certain level of service and support will be delivered. When customers pay a premium price for a product or service, they tend to expect a higher level of attention.

Customers who pay top dollar will be extremely disappointed to find that a customer service experience is not consistent with the high-end quality promised by the brand. Likewise, if your corporate brand is fresh, fun, and creative, the attitude presented through your support channels should reflect a similar perspective.

The way a customer experiences your brand goes far beyond service and support, extending to sales strategies, market decisions, and product selection. Branding is not simply a creative exercise. Building brand value requires a holistic approach to understanding customer expectations and experiences from top to bottom, inside and outside the organization.

Brand equity—the tangible value of your brand—can be increased exponentially when customer experience not only mirrors your brand, but also provides a living testimony to the attributes you aspire to embody.

Chapter 7

Indelible Brands

If you're going to build a strong brand for your business, a good place to start is by understanding the true nature of a brand.

I am not a proponent of the adage that "a brand is a promise." While I support the concept of a brand promise, the implied contract between a company and its customers, that idea that a brand *is* a promise is a little too simplistic for me.

Branding is not a one-way street. A brand does not become great without permission. Customers, employees, and prospects all need to accept the brand promise your company offers. If it is not believable, if your company isn't credible, all your branding efforts will fall flat.

What is a Brand?

That sounds like a simple question, but it's really not. There are thousands of perspectives and the whole idea can become thoroughly confusing for people who don't live and breathe marketing every day.

A good way to look at the concept is to envision a brand as an intersection. It's the place where the promise meets permission. Where that place is located depends as much on the desires of your company (brand vision) as it does on the acceptance of those who receive your brand messages (your audience).

Dialog and agreement are required create what I call the Permission Zone, where the essence of a brand comes to life. Figure 10 illustrates the way corporate or brand messages integrate with the views and assumptions of the audience that receives them. The intersection of these two is the Permission Zone.

Figure 10: The Permission Zone

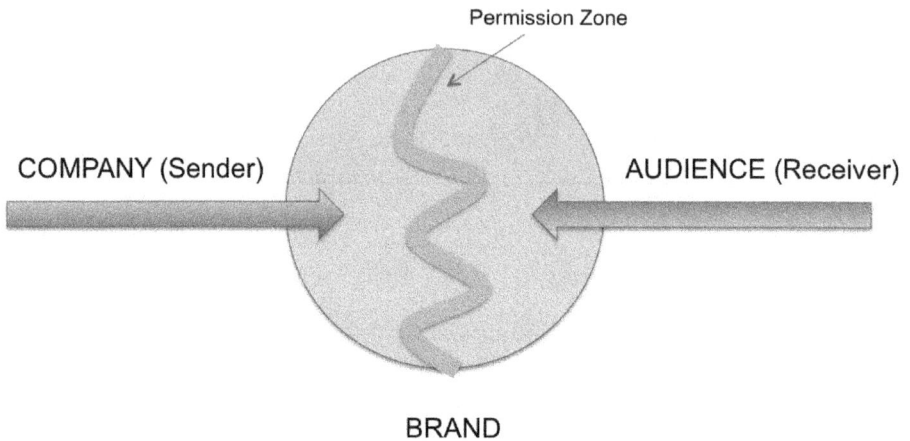

Listening to customers, understanding and anticipating their needs and desires, is vital to gaining their permission to create the brand you envision.

Once you understand your ideal customer, you know which brand attributes are relevant to them. You can create brand messages that appeal to this audience and design creative applications (collateral, advertising, websites) that express the right brand personality.

Then you're ready to meet your customer at the right intersection, instead of hanging out on a corner in the wrong neighborhood.

Why Brand Matters

Many businesses do not to take their brands as seriously as they should. Beyond basic brand identity (items like the look of a logo or the design of a website), attention to the core of a brand is often lacking. The whole concept of brand, what your company represents to the world, both in theory and in practice, should never be overlooked.

If you haven't paid much attention to your brand attributes, if you can't express your brand personality, if you do not have a vision for what your company represents, chances are your brand does not stand for much.

I've spent a lot of time working on brand positioning projects, helping companies define how they want to be seen. Understanding the space a company needs to occupy in its customers' minds and where they stand relative to competitors who are vying for the same mental real estate is critical to building a business with staying power. The only way to achieve this is through a deliberate thought process focused on defining the ideal brand for your constituents.

Some people have suggested that the whole idea of branding is old school, and they couldn't be more wrong. Consider, for example, the realm of social media. In our world of instant communications, social networks have the power to build or destroy a brand in hours, if not mere minutes.

We see it happen again and again when hapless employees or unhappy customers post comments or videos that inflame the media or go viral online, drawing attention to failings of the businesses or executives under scrutiny.

Knowing that social media is like a powder keg that, if ignited, has explosive and destructive power makes many managers fearful, even if they are comfortable with social media for personal use. This uncontrollable nature of online communities causes some cautious businesses to avoid social media altogether.

Control may be a bit much to expect, but businesses can and should seek to influence positive perceptions in their communities—online and off. Being proactive in this regard is a stronger strategic approach than hiding and hoping for the best (which rarely works out well).

The reality is that your business already has a brand image, whether you created it purposefully or not. If you abdicate responsibility for branding, avoiding communication with customers, people will form their own opinions. These opinions will vary radically from one person to the next, undermining brand value and eroding equity.

Lack of clarity or even confusion about what your brand stands for makes it more difficult to grow a business. Without a shared language to articulate your value, customers are hard pressed to express why someone should do business with you. If they do not know what to say about you, they likely won't say much. At least not much that is good.

Companies destined to thrive in the future recognize the value and power of word-of-mouth (WOM) marketing and make it work to their advantage with crystal-clear brand messages. They are not afraid to join the social conversation and they embrace the challenges of online reputation management as an opportunity to turn bad into good.

These companies know their brand, they can tell you what it represents, and they work hard to make sure that everyone knows where they stand. You should, too.

Passionate Brand Advocates

A strong brand can make the difference between winning a sale and losing it, commanding a premium price or selling at a discount. While this has been proven time and again through research, many executives (maybe you?) still question the value of branding, especially at budget time.

Building brand equity takes a sustained commitment and consistent investment in intangibles like relationships and awareness. Because influence, affinity and advocacy can seem ethereal, it's easier for executives to allocate scarce financial resources to more tangible alternatives like new equipment, facilities, hiring, or technology.

That is not always the best choice.

Brand affinity (a.k.a. "brand love") is not something you can touch, hold, or easily measure, but it does pay dividends just the same. Brand influence can distinguish your business from a host of competitors. The more passionate customers are about your brand, the greater the value differential between your business and others.

If you're not sure how to know when customers love your brand, here are five telltale signs:

Five Signs of Brand Love

Your most passionate brand advocates...

1. **Tell all their friends about you.** They're vocal ambassadors for your brand, spreading the word because they want their friends and associates to share in the experience of doing business with your company. Think of the last time you had a great meal at a new restaurant or played a spectacular golf course. Did you keep it to yourself, or share?

2. **Want more of a good thing.** When people trust your brand and enjoy the customer experience, they look forward to the opportunity to connect again and again. These customers eagerly anticipate the introduction of new products and services, like fans lining up to buy the latest product from Apple or a hot new game release.

3. **Overlook your shortcomings.** Every relationship has flaws and it's inevitable that eventually there will be misunderstandings or a miscommunication. This might spell the end of a customer relationship for companies with weak brands or a poor reputation. When you have passionate fans, small errors or missteps are likely to be forgiven. In fact, if you recover well, they'll love you even more.

4. **Look forward to a future together.** Like lifelong fans of pro sports teams, customers who love and trust a brand anticipate a long-term relationship. Even if they don't know what's around the next bend in their customer journey, they have faith you'll deliver on your commitment to meet their evolving needs and expectations.

5. **Make sacrifices to be with you.** Committed brand advocates look at purchases from your company as an investment. They will save

up their money, giving up other things to do business with you—even if it costs more. They don't mind stretching a bit to realize the benefits of being your customer, and they advise others to do the same.

A Better Bottom Line

All these signs translate into real bottom-line benefits for your business. You can quantify the impact of brand love when by measuring results like:

- Reduced customer churn

- Shorter sales cycles

- More accurate forecasting

- Premium pricing

- Higher profit margins

- Greater customer lifetime value

- Rapid adoption of new products

- Improved marketing ROI

I could add many more items to this list. Instead I'll challenge to you the think of a few of your own. How else will improving brand value transform your business?

Branding and the New Sales Cycle

As customers—both B2B and consumer alike—take more control of the buying process, the power of a brand relationship is more compelling than ever. Use this to your advantage and stand out from competitors.

The New Sales Funnel

Before people were empowered by digital access to product information, ratings, online discounts, and easy comparison shopping, the universe of choices was tightly controlled and carefully managed by sellers. Companies decided which products or services they wanted to promote, then their Sales and Marketing teams went to work to build awareness, create interest, and drive demand.

Now customers move themselves through the sales cycle, gathering information online, doing research, reading reviews, and so on. If and when a sales rep gets involved, it's often considerably later in the sales process when the buyer is much closer to making a selection.

The further along the process that first connection occurs, the less opportunity there is for sellers to influence decisions and build trusting relationships with buyers. This is especially true in the B2B world, where sales reps have traditionally been the ones to help customers navigate purchasing decisions, often keeping them focused on a limited universe of options.

A study by the Corporate Executive Board[14] found that B2B customers completed nearly 60% of a typical purchasing decision cycle before even having a conversation with a supplier. Buyers set requirements, researched solutions, ranked options, and compared pricing without even engaging a sales rep.

We see the impact of this shift in retail and consumer sales as well. Retail stores often serve as showrooms for customers who research products online and simply want to see or touch the merchandise before completing a transaction online.

Retailers are fighting back with strategies to counteract undercutting by online-only merchants. They are also embracing online channels of their own, encouraging shoppers to use a variety of resources to discover solutions and purchase products.

---

[14] Ana Lapter. 2011. *The Most Important Number in B2B Marketing*. CEB Marketing.

Sellers know that busy buyers love mobile devices like tablets and smartphones, and they're adapting their approach to facilitate a fluid, omni-channel experience that integrates stores, mobile and web-based capabilities.

Brand Makes a Difference

Both online and off, marketing efforts to build brand reputation and awareness are critical to shaping the decision process early on. It's brand that will get your company into the decision mix, and brand value that will keep you there throughout the evaluation process.

Building brand influence through online channels, using social media, branded display ads, and other digital strategies can distinguish your business from a host of competitors. Understanding the new buyer behavior and becoming part of the process can catapult your business to the top of a buyer's shopping list.

This doesn't mean being everywhere with excessive retargeting,[15] over the top email campaigns, or in-your-face pop up ads. Instead, you need to become an ally for buyers, helping them find the information they need to make smart decisions.

Content marketing with informative articles, videos, and objective reviews can fulfill a buyer's need for information while building credibility for your brand. Tactics like showcasing your product in use, providing relevant case studies, and offering feature comparison tools all enable allow prospects to do their homework while positioning your business as a trusted, go-to resource.

Take care to provide the appropriate information at each stage of the sales cycle instead of overwhelming prospects with too much information at once. Use a contextual approach that takes advantage of tools like marketing automation to deliver resources that move a buyer along their personal decision path until they're ready to connect with you one-on-one.

---

[15] Retargeting is a digital strategy that uses cookies and other technologies to place ads and offers in front of customers who have already browsed a site or researched a product or service. Retargeting can dramatically increase conversion rates.

Sales as Sherpa

Throughout the new decision process, sales representatives play an evolving role. Just as a Sherpa helps a mountain climber realize the benefits of all the training that happened before the climb, a sales representative must serve as an expert guide for a well-prepared client.

This relationship requires trust from the client, reinforced by the actions of the sales person. Educated customers often challenge sales staff on representations about their product. The response must be collaborative, not confrontational, gently guiding prospects to the correct information and building a stronger relationship along the way.

If your branding efforts have successfully engendered a foundation of trust, buyers will be more receptive to advice from a sales representative when the personal connection is finally made. Otherwise, they may be looking for a reason to rule you out of the mix, and an adversarial sales relationship will certainly do the trick.

Ultimately, the role of Sales is to help a buyer achieve their goal. It's a matter of asking, "Where do you want to go?" and "How can I help you get there?" instead of saying, "Here's where I believe you need to be."

Learn to Dance

Achieving success in the new sales cycle is a bit like learning an intricately choreographed dance. A standout performance requires careful coordination of sales, marketing and communications resources.

Buyers might not be ready to talk with you right away, but they yearn for the comfort of knowing that you're there for them. They want you as a seller to be ready and available to provide support when needed as they work towards the best buying decision.

You shouldn't step on their toes, but you also need to be ready to sweep them off their feet when the moment is right.

Buyers do this dance with companies and brands they can trust. Be dependable, deliver a brand they can count on, and you'll earn the privilege of leading prospects to the final sale.

Build a Better Brand

Many new businesses struggle with defining their brand identity, unsure of where to stake their claims in this rapidly changing landscape. Likewise, more established businesses have brand challenges of their own.

If you've been in business for a while, odds are good that your branding has gotten a little sloppy from advancing age or failure to stay current in the face of change all around.

To polish things up, try this simple three-step process for building a better brand:

Step 1: Conduct a Brand Audit

If it has been a while since you took an objective look at your brand, you might be surprised to discover brand value slipping away.

Over time and through use, revision, and interpretation, brand messages get diluted and visual identity elements like logos tend to be modified or misused.

Keep an eye out for these clues that signal it's time for your brand to get a facelift:

- **Muddy Messages**—If your brand message isn't crystal clear, it is not getting through.

- **Poor Positioning**—Your customers don't view you the way you want to been seen.

- **Clashing Communications**—Sales pitches, marketing messages and customer service scripts are out of sync.

- **Leaky Logos**—A tweak here, a touch up there. Before you know it, your logo has multiple looks and a watered-down image.

- **Bleeding Colors**—Close enough does not count when your corporate colors are concerned.

If any of these items sound familiar, it is time to take a closer look at the execution of your branding strategy and a brand audit is a good place to start. You can do an audit in-house, or hire a consultant to help you collect and assess the information that represents your current brand.

Here's the quick way to get a feel for your current brand status:

Go on a scavenger hunt and gather everything (yes, everything) you can find that represents your business. Collect brochures, sales presentations and articles about your company. Print out web pages, blog posts, and your Twitter history. Clip advertisements. Grab some business cards and letterhead. Find coupons, invoices, hang tags, promo items. Look at packaging, customer email templates and even take snapshots of building signage.

Once you have these materials in one place, spread them all out so you can get a good view. Use a conference table, a wall, or the floor to display everything where you can see it.

Step back and consider what these things say about your business, both visually and in the text. Is there a consistent theme, or are the messages all over the place?

Be objective. Does it all make sense? Make notes about what you see and what's missing. Some questions to answer include:

- Does your brand message come through clearly, or is it confusing?

- Do you have multiple messages, and some that compete or conflict with others?

- Is your visual image consistent, or do you have different logos, assorted colors, and a variety of looks?

- What does the overall image suggest about the brand personality of your business?

- What's not there? Are key messages absent?

Make notes about your impressions and then ask some objective outsiders (people who don't know your brand as well as you do) for their thoughts.

Step 2: Start Talking—and Listening

This step will help you get a fresh perspective on your brand. Get out of the office or get on the phone. Talk to customers and prospects. If you have distributors or retailers for your products, talk to them, too.

Here's what you need to know:

How do they see your business today? Does this match up with how you want them to view your company?

What do they like or dislike?

How would they describe your company to a peer?

Ask your constituents what they need or want from a company like yours. What do they wish you offered that's not in your mix?

Find out what they're not getting from your competitors, or how those competitors fall short of expectations. Their responses can be used to update your branding with new messages that resonate with your customers' current concerns.

If you're concerned about getting objective feedback, hire someone to interview your customers and prospects, taking detailed notes on what they learn. You might even want to do a little secret shopping to see for yourself what's working and what is not.

At the end of this step, ask yourself these questions...

- Does the experience you uncovered in this step match with the messages you found in your brand audit?

- What areas are the most divergent from your message, or your customers' expectations?

- Where does your message most closely match up with the customer experience or the desires of your prospects?

Document the gaps you identify. They will be used in the next step of the process to move your brand closer to where it needs to be.

Step 3: Get Organized for Action

In this final step, take all the information you've gathered and use it to update your brand. Focus on the most effective messages and visuals, and get rid of things that aren't working.

Don't be too sentimental in this phase. You will need to make some tough decisions about what to lose and what to keep:

- Do you need to update or change business processes to better reflect your brand?

- Is it time to cut a product that no longer fits your mix?

- Should you dump an ad campaign that does not send the right message?

Once you've done the pruning, add new items that reinforce your brand message. Anything you add to the mix must improve the consistency of your communications.

- Create a **messaging matrix** that outlines the key messages for your brand, along with supporting points. Use this as a guide when developing new marketing materials.

- Select a consistent **color palette** and graphic style for all your communications. Use a tone in your copy that supports the brand personality you want to express.

- Develop **brand standards** to govern how your logo is used. Specify what colors, fonts, and types of images should be used in your sales and marketing collateral.

Once you have all of these items in place, train your staff on how to use them, and do periodic checks to be sure they are applied uniformly throughout your organization. As you tackle new projects, think about how they reinforce or detract from your brand. Stay true to your plans, and you'll quickly build a better brand.

Differentiate, by Design

One of the best investments you can make in your business is to take the time to plan your desired customer experience before spending a dime on advertising or graphic design. That's why I put so much emphasis on understanding and articulating your brand.

What's it like to do business with your company? Everything from how you answer the phone to the way you thank customers for purchases is part of the customer experience. Every touch point, every impression, every nuance contributes to the overall experience, and it all influences perceptions of your brand.

Your business has a brand whether you planned it or not, and the same is true for customer experience. If you're open for business, you have already created a customer experience. It could be good or bad, but it's there all the same.

With this in mind, be intentional about making that experience the best it can be. Interactions with your business should be memorable (in a good way) so customers will come back again and be willing refer others to you.

To proactively define your customer experience, make notes about how you want a customer to feel before, during, and after interacting with your business.

- What's it like when you walk in the door?
- What happens after the sale?
- What emotions are associated with working with you?

Once you have established a solid understanding of your desired customer experience, use design to help you communicate the tenets of your brand at every touch point.

As a leader, you should drive the process of connecting experience and brand. This is a strategic exercise, so don't cede important decisions to an agency or designer who doesn't know your business as well as you do.

Provide a clear vision for your designers, enabling them to generate creative ideas that effectively bring your brand vision to life. Pull together a team of specialized professionals for interior design, packaging, products, websites and graphics (the exact mix will depend on the nature of your business).

Share the details of your desired customer experience with them, and be open to a variety of ideas that evoke the emotional response you want. Creating a strong identity is a smart business investment.

Think Beyond the Logo

Your desired customer experience should inform decisions about things like signage, packaging, and even layout of your physical space if customers come to your location.

The tactile feel of materials and even scents can be important in addition to visual considerations. Color matters in terms of evoking a restful or energetic impression, but consistency in applying the design is equally important.

Echoing things like a shape or an icon can reinforce the image and experience. For example, an arch or a curve can be repeated in the shape of a bag, in the background of wall graphics, and on dressing room doors, or employee apparel.

I have a client that has done this very effectively with a stylized dragonfly that is part of their logo, but also appears etched on glass in their office, in the background of their website and other places where the image subtly reinforces the brand.

In retail, this idea can be used in packaging—bags, gift wrap, samples, hangtags, coupons, etc. Applying design themes to things like ribbons, cards, and tissue paper works well to build an experience.

An affordable alternative to custom items is to find off—the-shelf colors and materials that contribute to the overall image. For businesses on a budget, investing in more highly visible items or those with broader use like multi-purpose note cards can be cost-effective.

Finally, be a vigilant guardian of your brand. Use your logo, colors, and fonts consistently everywhere you can. That means no spin-offs or modifications of the original design. Stretched, skewed, or "almost" right color logos will hurt branding efforts.

Being obsessive about design and branding will save lots of money in the long run, creating a positive customer experience and a strong foundation for your marketing.

When to Redesign Your Logo

How do you know when it is time to update your company's logo? Changing an established corporate identity has risks—and rewards.

Surprisingly, the age of your logo is irrelevant when deciding to make a change. Some logos are timeless; others need to be updated every few years. Why the difference? Your logo represents your brand, and your brand reflects the positioning of your company. If your business changes rapidly to meet market conditions or incorporate new technologies, logo revisions may be warranted more frequently.

Here are some clues that it might be time to change your logo:

Entering new markets

If your company is moving into new markets, reaching out to new customer segments or expanding geographically, an updated logo might better reflect your current target markets. Have you moved from local to global? Your logo might still indicate a smaller horizon that does not match your goals.

Changes in product lines

Have you added or discontinued major product lines? There may be elements of your logo that imply product attributes that no longer match your offerings. If that's the case, a design refresh might be in order to help your brand communicate a more streamlined or expansive product set.

Industry evolution

As technology changes in your industry, you may come to see that your logo is tied to an outdated trend. Putting a fresh face on your company can be a good signal that your business is changing with the times and embracing innovations.

Shifting customer expectations

Customer needs change over time. As more competitors enter an industry, their messages can skew customer perceptions and change expectations about your business. You might need to address these changes with a logo design that differentiates your business and embraces customers' current desires.

Modified business model

Major changes in the way you do business, such as shifts in pricing strategy or a different method of delivering products and services can transform your company. When dramatic changes are made, it makes sense to telegraph these changes with your corporate identity.

Now, you won't want to update your logo every time your business experiences one of these changes. But they do suggest when it's a good time to check your brand identity and make sure it matches your current business. If not, update your brand strategy and develop a logo and corporate identity that better reflects not only where you are now, but also where you want your business to be in the future.

Chapter 8

Magnetic Marketing

Marketing is Not a Faucet

Business owners and executives always hope their marketing invest-ments will pay off big. Once the strategy is done, plans are made, and vendors are lined up to help with execution, what could possibly go wrong?

Unfortunately, the answer is, "A lot."

While the list of potential hiccups is long, the single greatest contribu-tor to marketing failures is not unresponsive customers or competitive challenges. What undermines successful marketing most frequently is one simple factor: lack of commitment.

The biggest risk to your carefully created plans appears when doubt creeps in and commitment to begin to waver. You might assume that waning commitment to marketing programs happens when results are slow to appear. That's often the case, yet many executives place so much emphasis on monthly metrics and quarterly results that they fail to give marketing efforts adequate time to bear fruit.

Is the problem that your marketing really doesn't work, or does your marketing fail to deliver because you're too impatient and expect immediate results?

If you have suffered a frustrating string of "failures" it would pay to spend some time looking at the patterns that lead to them.

Like a cake plucked from the oven too soon, marketing results that are rushed can seem half-baked. The cake won't be edible and you'll be equally disappointed in what you perceive is wasted marketing expense. Suppress that discouragement for a moment and ask if your expectations are realistic.

There's nothing wrong with pulling the plug when you have solid evidence that things are not working out. In fact, I encourage cutting your losses rather than throwing good money away. When you discover that some of your assumptions were off the mark or that decisions on pricing or positioning missed the target, regroup quickly and move on.

However, if you are constantly itching to see a bigger impact or are eager to accelerate results, the problem could be you. The passion, drive, and focus that make an entrepreneur successful can also translate into a level of impatience that undermines the effectiveness of some marketing strategies.

Here are a few examples of areas when a drive for quick success can hurt…

Building brand awareness and establishing customer preference can take time. Customers needs to learn about your business, try your offerings, and learn to trust your promises.

Referral programs are long-term affairs. They require satisfied customers who are willing to spread the word, leading to a ripple effect of expanding recommendations to new prospects and customers.

Lead generation campaigns yield better results when paired with nurturing programs to ensure slow moving opportunities aren't overlooked. Some leads need to be nurtured for months or even years before converting to sales.

Integrated marketing marries branding, social media and traditional marketing. It can have an exponential impact on results…over time. Campaigns rarely result in an overnight sensation.

For these reasons, you should never try to turn marketing on and off like a faucet. Doing so interrupts the momentum that builds with a sustained commitment to marketing. Stopping and starting programs on a whim (or to meet short-term financial metrics) usually has a negative impact on results, dragging down the overall ROI of your marketing investments.

If you really want to see better marketing results, commit yourself to following through on planned marketing efforts, even those that do not show immediate returns. Tweak programs as needed, but do not turn your budget on and off to meet capricious benchmarks.

Think of marketing as a "buy and hold" type of investment. Rebalance the portfolio occasionally, but do not tinker incessantly. Have faith in your strategy and be dogged in your execution. Your business will benefit from the compound interest and you'll reap bigger dividends in the end.

Winning Referrals

Referral marketing is important in any business, although some depend on referrals more than others. If your business is in an industry where new buyers are unfamiliar with the top service providers, where the personal relationship between service provider and customer is critical, where the decision process is cumbersome and confusing, or the risk of making the wrong decision is high, you're in a referral business.

Some of the most common types of referral-driven businesses are:

- Health care providers (doctors, dentists, chiropractors)

- Home repair and improvement (contractors, remodeling, plumbing, electrical)

- Home building or purchase and enhancement (real estate, architects, interior design)

- Personal services (hair care, nails, massage, waxing)

- Financial services (life insurance, financial planning, CPAs, banking, mortgage)

- Automotive (auto repair, body work, auto insurance, driver training)

- Education (tutors, test prep, college advisors, private schools)

- Professional services (consulting, accountants, attorneys, bankers)

The common theme here is that each decision carries an element of risk, whether the investment is large (a mortgage) or small (a haircut). Buyers are taking a leap of faith when choosing providers, hoping that the company they select will provide a quality service and won't rip them off.

Because trust is such an integral part of the decision process, customers in these segments often seek out referrals before making a decision. In order to be the company that is referred by a buyer's friends, family, and acquaintances, it is critical for you to maintain not only an outstanding reputation, but also top-of-mind awareness.

What is a Good Referral?

Not all referrals are quality referrals. In fact, getting too many introductions to the wrong kind of prospects can cause a problem. It takes valuable time to vet prospects, and you want to reserve this time for the most qualified opportunities.

Telling a referral that you can't meet their needs because you're too busy creates the potential for reputation-damaging discontent. To avoid this problem, you must frame your requests for referrals in the right context. Your customers and business contacts need to know who your ideal prospects are so they can share information about you with people who will most benefit from working with you.

If you're working through this book in sequence, you have already identified a target customer profile. Use this profile to express to clients and referral sources the types of customers you are best able to help. Work in key elements that suggest who your ideal clients are, highlighting your value proposition to show why they choose you.

As an example, here are some things the owner of a home improvement firm might say:

"We work with busy homeowners who live in neighborhoods like Walden Woods and need to update their aging homes. Our clients appreciate our ability to make remodeling a quick and easy experience, and they value the high-quality we deliver in the finished product."

It can also be beneficial to cite supplemental information for added context, such as…

"Most of our home renovation projects are in the $50,000-75,000 range…"

"We often work with single homeowners who don't have time to manage their own subcontractors."

"Our clients know what they want, and we collaborate with them to make their vision a reality."

Note: Although the concept is similar, this approach is not an "elevator pitch." It's a positioning process designed to help you connect with the best possible prospects for your business.

Create a Referral Culture

At first it may feel awkward or uncomfortable to ask clients for referrals. As you build a referral culture in your company, it will become second nature to you and your team.

A "referral culture" means that everything you do—from great service to quality products and timely delivery—is done with the intent that customers will be so satisfied that they are pleased to refer you. Every job, every interaction, should be worthy of a referral.

This culture extends to how you handle unhappy customers, which paradoxically are a great source of qualified referrals. Addressing a concern, error, or problem gracefully will endear clients to you. They will tell others about how well you handled, "...my problem with the dishwasher that died a week after it was installed."

Most people understand that problems happen, and your aim is not to have a completely error-free experience. That's an unrealistic goal. Instead, when issues do come up, rise to the challenge of handling them diplomatically. Resolving concerns by creating mutual satisfaction is the mark of an exceptional service provider.

Instill this customer-centered philosophy in your employees and any subcontractors you use, and you will have the foundation for a sustainable referral culture.

Referral Classes

In building a referral system, you want to encourage referrals from all sources, not just past customers. Think of three classes or circle of referral sources extending from this core base of clients, as illustrated in the diagram here:

Figure 11

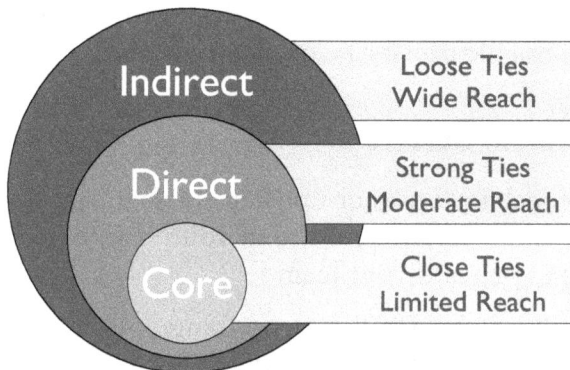

Your best referrals will come from the **Core**. These are people who know your work first hand and can attest to the value of working with you. This is also (usually) the smallest group of referral sources.

At times, clients are reticent to provide a referral for fear of losing exclusive access to you or for reasons such as confidentiality. With this in mind, it is critical to expand your reach and encourage referrals from a wider variety of sources.

The second circle is **Direct**. These are the people who know you personally, though you haven't personally done work for them. They can be strong referral sources, if you remind them regularly that you depend on referrals and ensure they know who your best prospects are.

Your direct referral circle includes people like business partners and associates, as well as neighbors, social contacts and professionals you do business with (think of your CPA, attorney and others). With this group, being top of mind is important.

Finally, **Indirect** referrals give you the broadest reach, but also have the loosest ties. Indirect referrals come from people who have heard of you, but haven't met you or don't know you well. These people will remember you based on your reputation and what they have heard from others, such as their neighbors, business associates, and friends.

Build your referral system to address all three of these groups, making it easy for them to remember and refer you when the opportunity arises.

Key Factors in Getting Referrals

As you are working on developing your referral business, keep in mind these three factors. Each is essential to your reputation as a referral-worthy business. If you consistently fall short in any area, referrals will dry up. People who give you referrals never want to hear, *"I called that woman you recommended, and I never heard back."*

Be Likeable—People are more likely to refer someone they like. Being friendly, personable and taking time to get to know people on a personal level (interests, family, job situation) will generate more referrals than being "strictly business."

Be Reachable—Making it easy for people to get in touch with you encourages referrals. Offering a number of ways for people to contact you, from phone to email, helps. It's also useful to be known for answering the phone when you can, being accessible and approachable.

Be Responsive—This is tied to being reachable, because if people can't connect with you on the first try, you need to follow-up quickly. Being responsive also entails following up quickly on problems and concerns, and going the extra mile to show you care.

As you balance service delivery with the day-to-day demands of business development and running your company, you may find that some of these items can be challenging. Fortunately, you can implement systems that make it appear easy, such as:

- **CRM (customer relationship management) systems** to capture a wide range of details about clients and track interactions with prospects.

- **Virtual phone systems** can route office calls to your cell when you choose, or send transcriptions of voice messages via email or text message.

- **Response metrics.** Set expectations on how and when you respond to inquiries. For example, tell customers if you "typically return all calls and emails within 24 hours."

Service Recovery

While you may strive to provide a seamless experience for customers, that's not always possible. No matter how hard you try, problems will occasionally crop up. When this happens, rising to the challenge and handling problems diplomatically, resolving them with mutual satisfaction can be the mark of an exceptional professional.

Here are some tips to smooth the way when problems arise:

- Apologize promptly, even if the issue was not your fault.

- Take ownership of finding a solution.

- Avoid criticism or placing blame.

- Provide options. "We have a couple of ways to handle this. Would you prefer A or B?"

- Confirm that the outcome was satisfactory in your client's view.

Referral Generation Strategies

There are a number of activities that will help you build a pipeline of qualified referrals. These do not all need to be tackled at once, but over time you will want to create a robust system of activities that support referral generation.

In isolation, these tactics will yield merely average results. The real power and impact on your referral flow comes when you employ a methodical, persistent approach to implementation. To achieve this, pick two or three of the following items to start. Then, add more and refine your approach over time.

When measuring the results of referral general programs, resist the temptation to single out one element to which you attribute success or failure.

It will be hard to determine which activity contributed the most to a referral, since the system requires that all your programs work in concert. Look at the overall impact on your referral rate, and make changes in small steps, such as increasing or decreasing the level or intensity of a given tactic.

Keep-in-touch programs

Staying in touch consistently is the number one thing you can do to inspire referrals. People don't refer someone they don't remember. Make sure they remember you by touching base regularly.

There are many options for staying in touch with contacts, whether they are past customers or simply people you know from your day-to-day interactions.

Personal Calls

Keep-in-touch calls are a valuable way to stay connected with your best referral sources. Setting up a system to help you remember who to call when can greatly simplify the process.

You may want to call a contact six months after a purchase, or reach out to a referral source every quarter to catch up. Decide on a routine that works for you, and create a task or calendar reminder. A report from your CRM or contact management system can make this easy, providing names and numbers to call on a regular basis.

This process does not need to be a major time commitment; even a simple voice mail can be effective. Schedule an hour or so each week to make calls to the top priority contacts, and you'll see results in terms of greater engagement and more referrals.

Greeting Cards or Personal Notes

Occasional greetings are a good way to stay in touch with past customers and close contacts—if done well. Unlike generic cards, sincere greetings require a personal touch. They should include details that show you care about the relationship, with a short one-line note and a signature rather than your printed name.

Cards can be sent to recognize birthdays or major events such as promotions, client anniversaries or holidays. You can choose completely custom cards, store bought greetings or something in between.

Cards can be sent to recognize:

Birthdays—An approach frequently used by Realtors® and insurance agents.

Anniversaries—This can be a personal date like a wedding anniversary, or one directly related to your business, such as when you started working together.

Holidays—Greeting for traditional holidays or quirky dates to remember (maybe "Talk Like a Pirate" day) can be memorable.

Services like Send Out Cards and Cards for Your Clients can handle this for you at a cost comparable to that of purchasing cards at a retail store. You can also use a virtual assistant (VA) to hand address and mail cards that you sign personally.

Helpful Tips

Periodic emails or mailings of printed newsletter can provide useful information for customers, while allowing you to stay top-of-mind on a monthly, semi-monthly or quarterly basis.

Any tips should relate to your business without being too sales-oriented. The goal is to be seen as an expert resource, so the more valuable the information you provide, the better.

As an example, here some informative articles a home improvement business might share with its customers:

> *Keeping Kitchen Cabinets "Like New"*
>
> *Better, Brighter Grout — How to Care for Those Pesky Grout Lines*
>
> *Repair or Replace? When to Upgrade Your Appliances*

If you want to set yourself apart from the mass of promotional emails that land in inboxes these days, try a printed newsletter instead. Most people don't get nearly as much mail as they used to, so a well-done, informative newsletter can stand out.

Create it yourself or use a customized newsletter service. There are many industry-specific offerings that incorporate your company news with articles of a more general nature. These firms handle the editing, layout, printing, and mailing to make the process easier for you.

There are also a number of firms you can use to develop a completely custom newsletter or tip sheet (a two-sided sheet to be sent with a personal cover letter).

Gratitude

Expressing gratitude to customers and partners is a wonderful way to encourage referrals. Being appreciative elevates your firm as professional and friendly, a pleasure to work with.

If you're in a service business, seize every opportunity tell customers, "Thanks," as part of your referral strategy:

Thank clients for referrals with a call, email, or handwritten note.

Thank prospects for meeting with you. Send a hand-written card mailed the day after an initial meeting.

Thank customers for considering you. Even if you don't get the account, say, "Thanks for considering us. If we can help you in the future, please don't hesitate to give us a call."

Say "Thank you" at the end of a big project with an appropriate gift that relates to your work. A kitchen designer might offer:

- A gift basket full of kitchen gadgets
- A gourmet picnic basket
- A wine and cheese platter or cheese board and knife set.

Be sure to include a personal, hand-signed note: "We hope you enjoy your new kitchen. Here's a small token of our appreciation..." These items should be of high quality to reinforce your brand image.

Neighborhood or community marketing

For local businesses targeting a highly defined geographic area, outreach to the community can generate lots of referrals. If appropriate for your business (for instance, restaurants, home remodeling, kitchen design, real estate, etc.), communicating with neighbors is a wonderful way to build your reputation and generate referrals.

When possible, take the opportunity to make a positive impression by contributing to the community and becoming well known. Note that you are not necessarily asking for business. Don't be the creepy guy who knocks on the door and says, *"We're working in the area, and would like to offer you a quote for a new roof."*

Instead, use more subtle messages that demonstrate your professionalism and expertise in your field. These attributes encourage referrals even from people who have not used your services, because you have made a positive first impression.

If you're not sure how this approach could work for your business, consider this sequence of communications that a swimming pool company could use:

1. Send a **"We're getting started letter"** to let neighbors know you'll be working on their street. This is not a letter to solicit business. The core message is, "We don't want to cause an inconvenience, so if you have any concerns, please give us a call."

2. **During a long project**, send an update letter to let neighbors know how it's going. Point out how projects like a high-end pool and related landscaping can improve home values in the neighborhood. The letter assures neighbors again that you don't want to be disruptive, and that you are available to address any problems or concerns.

3. **At the end of a project**, send a simple postcard to let neighbors know the project is complete. Thank them for their patience, and let them know you'd be happy to help them if they are considering a similar project. With your client's permission, include photos of the completed pool area.

If direct mail seems like too much work, outsource it. The U.S. Postal Service can simplify mailings to large neighborhoods or areas with over 200 addresses using their Every Door Direct Mail service.

This approach can also be used in a business-to-business model or by businesses that reach beyond a local market. Look at the community you serve and find creative ways to highlight your activities.

Articles in association newsletters, presentations at industry events and volunteering on committees are all ways to be visible and generate referrals from your industry community.

Sponsorships

Sponsorships of local programs and teams (or industry and association events if your business is B2B), can keep your company top-of-mind, increasing the chances that your name will be the one that comes up when people ask friends and colleagues, "Do you know someone who does _____?"

For businesses serving consumers in a local market, high schools provide a wonderful opportunity for affordable sponsorships. These can be found through the school's athletic booster clubs or simply by calling the office.

You may also be able to sponsor or advertise in the school's theater productions or art shows. In some cases, signage is available at the athletic fields in addition to logo or ad placement in printed programs. Community swim or tennis teams and local chambers of commerce also offer sponsorship opportunities.

Regardless of which sponsorship venues you choose, consistency is important. Try to be more visible in a clearly defined area rather than diluting your efforts by trying to cover too large an area. A concentrated approach gives you a greater frequency of impressions, and this higher level of visibility leads to more referrals.

(For more on Sponsorships, see Successful Sponsorships *on page 165.)*

Build credibility

As you build awareness for your business, you will enjoy a certain amount of credibility from the implied endorsement that comes with a referral. At the same time, prospects will check you out, and you need to validate what they have heard with additional credibility signals. (Online, this is called social proof, referring to the fact that others prove you are who and what you claim to be.)

Testimonials—Use customer quotes on your website and in your marketing and promotional materials. In addition, capture testimonials on online review sites, LinkedIn or other websites suited to your line of business.

News—Positive press coverage serves as an endorsement for your business. Keep your eyes open for opportunities to talk with media representatives, have your projects showcased, or provide tips and advice.

Online Reviews—Buyers looking for reputable companies often read online reviews on sites like Amazon, Service Magic, Angie's List, Manta, BBB, etc. If there are sites specific to your industry, claim your company profile so that you can provide current and correct product and contact information.

Being active on review sites will also help you stay in tune with what people are saying, so you can be proactive in addressing any concerns that bubble up.

Content Marketing

For years we've heard that content is king, and businesses around the world have been listening. The growth of social media has provided a platform for distribution of content like never before, and companies are churning out articles, blogs, white papers, videos, webinars and other content at a record pace.

So what's the problem?

Not many years ago, what we now call "content" was produced by analysts, researchers, writers, and journalists who spent a great deal of time developing well-written, thoughtful, and provocative material. This material was published for readers who had a deep and genuine interest in the topic at hand.

From exploring new vendors and service offerings to researching competitors and market opportunities, consumers of this content could be reasonably confident that what they downloaded would be worth their time—and the price of their email address or contact information.

These days, cranking out content has almost become an end in itself. For many marketers, content is simply a sales hook designed to capture email addresses and generate leads. Frequently, there is little concern about offering a quality product, as long as the goal of building the email list is achieved. The result is a whole lot of digital noise.

It is becoming more and more difficult to find quality content within the cacophony on the web. That's not because there is no great content available. In fact, there is plenty of good content being published every day. The problem is finding the gems in the midst of everything else. Discovering high quality content can be a huge task.

The sea of mediocrity and the frustration of locating valuable information may eventually kill the intense demand that made content marketing so popular in the beginning. It's kind of like the kid who loves chocolate until he has the chance to eat all his Halloween candy at once. He soon discovers that getting too much of what you want can be worse than not enough!

Don't Be Part of the Problem

Publishing content can be an integral part of a "thought leadership" strategy in which you position yourself or key employees as go-to experts in your field.

The key to making this effective is publishing valuable content and items of interest that can't easily be found elsewhere. If you do not follow this advice and randomly push out materials without thinking twice about the value they add, you could be part of the problem...and erode your brand.

If you're just regurgitating something you read elsewhere, stop. Instead, use items you like as inspiration to offer your own unique spin or position on a topic.

As you develop content for your business, make sure you are adding something meaningful to the universe of existing materials. Consider your audience and their needs. What will readers get in return for the time they spend with your content?

Provide a unique perspective, fresh insights or data from your own research. Offer information to help your readers improve their situation, solve problems, be more informed or become better educated.

Curate Carefully to Cultivate a Following

Just as powerful as creating content is the process of curating content. This simply means discovering great content—including articles, videos, infographics or research—and passing it along to others through channels such as social media.

If you think about the difference between visiting a flea market and a great museum, you'll understand why the quality of the collection matters. Be discriminating and don't blindly share content without reading it first. (That can be dangerous to your reputation!)

Before you retweet, share, or post content from other sources, review it. Yes, that means take the time to actually click on the link, read the article and decide: "Is it really good?" Would you recommend it to a friend or customer you were meeting with face-to-face? If not, hold out for something better.

A little restraint in curating the content you share will not only slow the spread of mindless stuff, if will also reflect positively on you. Carefully picking what to share—whether you write it yourself or promote content from other sources—will establish your position as an intelligent thought leader, someone who knows what's of value, and what's not.

Blogging for Business

Over the past several years, business blogs have become one of the primary vehicles for content marketing. At the same time, many businesses have started blogs only to see them gather dust as attention eventually turns to other more pressing matters.

Having a blog can be an excellent way to attract website traffic if you are committed to it. Well-written articles can build credibility and demonstrate expertise, helping you to differentiate your business from competitors.

Does Your Business Need a Blog?

Because of the perceived pressure to start a blog, business owners often ask me, "Do I really need a blog?" and my answer is usually, "It depends."

Every company is different, so determining the answer to the blogging question requires careful assessment. To see if your organization is ready to take on the blogging challenge, take this quick, five-step quiz.

Blog readiness test

1. **Are you genuinely interested in writing a blog?** Do you really want to blog or would you just be doing it because you've heard that you should? If you don't want to write blog posts yourself, are you willing to allocate resources from your team or hire someone who can bring passion to your blog?

2. **Are you committed to blogging consistently?** Whether your posts come monthly, weekly, or even daily, you need a predictable blogging schedule. You can plan ahead and post later, as long as you establish a pattern your readers can depend on. Adding new posts on a regular basis will attract a loyal following of readers for your blog.

3. **Do you have something to say?** You do not need to have earth-shattering insights, but a unique point of view and interesting perspectives are important to the success of your blog. Repeating the same old information that can be found anywhere online only adds to the noise in the blogosphere. Add value instead.

4. **Do you have the skills or resources required to optimize your blog?** Maximizing the reach and impact of your blog takes some know-how. From selecting keywords to design and SEO, getting the most from your blogging efforts may require you to gain some additional skills—either by learning them yourself or getting outside help.

5. **Do you know what your audience wants to read?** Blogging isn't really about promoting your company. It's about giving your readers the kind of content they want. What information and ideas can you share to make readers happy that they took the time to read your blog? If you don't know who your readers are or what they are interested in, find out before you start blogging.

What's your score?

Count the number of questions you answered with "Yes" and check your score:

>   *1-2: Wait and See.* A blog might not be for you—at least not yet. Revisit the idea when you can answer affirmatively to more of these questions (It's better to wait that to start too soon.)

>   *3-4: Give it a Try.* If you're committed, go ahead and give blogging a try. Set specific objectives for content and frequency of posts, and get help with formatting or writing when needed.

>   *5: Go for It.* You have all the pieces in place and it sounds like you are more than ready to blog. Develop a strategy to address when to post, who will write posts and edit them, and what content to cover and you'll be off and running.

Before you start

Are you convinced that now's the perfect time to start a blog for your business? If you think you're ready to tackle the challenge, here are a few things to consider before you start:

Blogging is hard. It's true. Creating a good, engaging, consistent blog is tough. It's not impossible, but it takes dedication and a willingness to learn in order to be successful. Are you ready for that?

Blogging is not free. Yes, you can set up a blog at WordPress.org, Blogger or some other platform without a penny down. But what is your time worth?

Are you willing to invest several hours a week to write blog posts, research new ideas, and respond to comments? What about finding images to dress up your posts? Think about how often you plan to post, and how much time you can commit.

Bloggers need a unique perspective. With hundreds of thousands of blogs out there, you do not want to be just one more small voice in a big crowd. You must have a distinctive take on your topic of choice.

If you are going to start a blog about personal fitness, world travel, or model trains, what insights can you offer to make your blog more appealing than the rest? Do you have unique experiences to share, a quirky or humorous point of view? If so, let it shine.

Blogging requires passion. If you're not passionate about the topics you are blogging about, your apathy will show. No one wants to read a post from someone who does not really care about the topic. What could be more boring than that?

Give your readers a reason to keep coming back to your blog by blogging about something that interests you. Be sure your passion won't wane after an initial rush of enthusiasm, like a love affair gone wrong. Blogging is like marriage, and that means a long-term commitment.

Blogging rarely make one an overnight success. It's rare for a blogger to enjoy a sudden rise to fame. The first few months, or even years, of a blog can feel like an eternity. You post. You wait for comments. You post again. Nothing happens. Don't worry; it's probably not you.

Building a following for a blog does not just happen, it takes time. It's a gradual process of spreading the word, providing quality posts, sharing them, then doing it all again. A retweet or "like" from someone influential can help, but be ready to keep plugging away instead of giving up in frustration.

If you've made it through this list and you're not discouraged, good for you! You have what it takes to be a successful blogger. If you're still not sure, give it some thought before deciding.

Successful Sponsorships

Are you thinking about sponsoring an event, conference, trade show or community fundraiser? Investing in sponsorships like these is a bit of a gamble.

If you're smart about the process, sponsorships can pay off, but often, they don't meet expectations. How can you avoid disappointment and turn this potential money pit into a real opportunity to build your business?

Like any other marketing investment, the decision to become a sponsor deserves careful consideration before you sign on. Here's how to evaluate your options to ensure you make the right call.

What's in It for You?

You can't effectively evaluate a sponsorship opportunity without understanding how it fits your goals. Start by looking at what you need to accomplish rather than what the organizer wants from you.

Even if the cause is dear to you, you must first consider your objectives so you can ensure they are met. The three main reasons to sign on for a sponsorship opportunity are:

1. You are focused on soft objectives. Do you want to increase visibility or build awareness within a highly targeted market, like a local community or a specific niche within your industry?

2. You have clearly measurable goals. Launching a new product or generating demand and capturing leads for a service offering would qualify.

3. You want to create goodwill. Supporting a community can position your business as a good corporate citizen or make it easier to recruit great employees, for example.

Determining which of these goals is most important to you should be your primary decision. Next, ask yourself if the sponsorship you are considering will help you achieve that objective.

Is It the Right Crowd?

Does the audience provided by the sponsorship align with your target prospects? If it is a community event, how many of the attendees are likely to be interested in your business? For industry sponsorships and trade groups, are the people participating really decision makers or influencers?

It's imperative that you reach the right people to get any financial return from the sponsorship. Don't hesitate to ask organizers for details about the job functions, interest areas or roles of past or prospective attendees.

Before agreeing to be a sponsor, find out how many people are expected to participate and get demographic information to be sure it matches your target prospects. Ask for attendee numbers, member counts, website visitors, etc.

If the event is not brand new, this information should be readily available. For trade shows, you may even be able to get an audited report on prior year participation.

Next, look closely at how the sponsorship will help you meet your goals. For example, if you want to build awareness for your business, consider how your company be represented and how much visibility you will get.

- Will your company be listed on event signage?

- Will the organizer publish your logo and a link to your website?

- Will your sponsorship be mentioned in publicity, presentations or printed programs?

- Can you distribute coupons and flyers to participants?
- Are there other value-added opportunities you can take advantage of? (There may be an extra free.)

If there will not be enough quality impressions (views of your brand name) then either pass up the opportunity or ask for more value to be added to your sponsorship package. Remember, everything is negotiable.

Document Sponsorship Agreements

Get all commitments in writing as part of your sponsorship agreement, especially if you've negotiated something that is not part of the standard package.

Sometimes the sales pitch includes verbal offers like, "We'll give you top billing on the signage," or "You'll be included in at least three press releases." Make sure all these promises are documented so you have something to fall back on if those commitments are not fulfilled.

You also need to know what will happen if the event is cancelled. Ask these questions in advance to avoid potential problems later. As they say, "Get it writing."

Get Involved

Rarely is it possible to simply write a check and get a big payoff from sponsorships. Success requires your involvement before, during, and after the event or program to get the most value from your investment.

Take into account any added costs and resources required. Are you expected to provide giveaways or have a personal presence with a tabletop display or exhibit booth? Do you need to send someone to speak as part of a panel presentation? If so, can your business support these requirements?

Do you need to submit graphics or other marketing materials that you have not yet created? What will that cost? These extra expenses are not usually included in the cost of the sponsorship package. Create a budget so you can determine your real costs before making a decision.

It takes work to leverage sponsorship opportunities for maximum return. This work extends beyond the event itself. Plan to follow-up after the fact to connect with leads and respond to inquires from people who expressed an interest in your business. Otherwise, your efforts will have been wasted.

Time for a Payoff

Finally, how quickly do you need to see a return from this investment? If your objective is building brand awareness, bear in mind that this is a long process, requiring consistent effort over time. It will take more than one event to accomplish.

If you are sponsoring an event with the hope of immediately increasing sales, you need to have a specific offer with a compelling call to action. Define in advance how you will track sales back to the event so you can evaluate the ROI.

Response codes, event-specific offers, or QR codes on coupons and flyers can help link inquiries to the sponsorship. Providing a unique web address or landing page for prospects is another good way to trace traffic back to an event or sponsorship campaign.

Keep it Going

Evaluate each sponsorship opportunity and decide if the results were worth the investment and effort. Would you do it again? If so, you may be able to secure a discount for signing on early for the next year or season. You may also be able to take advantage of year-round promotions that latecomers won't get.

Continue to leverage the contacts you made from the sponsorship through email marketing and other engagement tools like social media. Use your contact list to reach out to attendees for the next event—even if they haven't bought from you, they can generate referrals or become future customers. Don't let the seeds of the relationship you've planted dry up. Keep nurturing them and your sponsorship investment will grow.

Chapter 9

Digital Marketing Mastery

No matter what business you're in, a strong case can be made that it should be online. The world has gone digital and even the most low-tech industries are leveraging the Internet and mobile technology to connect with customers.

Because being online is all but mandatory, business growth often depends on mastering the ever-changing nuances of digital marketing. From web design to online advertising, SEO (search engine optimization) to reputation management, you need digital tools and resources to succeed.

To give you a jump-start, we'll cover the essential elements here, starting with a business-critical component: your website. We'll also cover SEO, digital advertising and social media.

What Does Your Website Say About You?

If you're not sure how to answer this question, go take a quick look. I'll wait...

What do you think? Do you love it? Are the graphics awesome? Is it all jazzed up with video or interactive tools? Were you disappointed? Maybe your site looks dated and needs a refresh. Was it so slow to load that you gave up and came right back here?

I'm often amazed by what businesses allow to represent them online. From outdated sites to ones that are impossible to read, it seems that sometimes companies forget that their site is out there, 24x7, for the entire world to see.

Like abandoned blogs that haven't been updated in months, I occasionally come across websites that clearly aren't active or pages that were moved with no forwarding address (the old "404: Page Not Found" error I'm sure you've encountered).

Some business sites are perpetually "coming soon" and others are always "down for maintenance." If that sounds familiar, it's high time for a website intervention!

Your company website is the digital storefront or office space for your business. Do you really want customers to think you've lost interest or closed up shop?

Why You Still Need a Website

Every now and then I hear someone argue that business websites are no longer necessary. Some companies—especially small business—are so enamored with social media that they have decided websites don't matter anymore. "We have a blog," they say, or "You can find us on Facebook."

What's wrong with that?

First, depending on social media sites for your online presence creates unnecessary risk for your business. Do you really want to risk not owning your digital property? Relying on social media is simply renting space and you can be evicted at any time.

Secondly, a social-only strategy can cause you to miss out on critical opportunities to connect with customers and prospects. People look to websites to learn about a company, validating that a business is "real" and viable.

In a sea of constant digital change, your website can demonstrate stability, continuity and reliability. Use it to differentiate your business, create trust, and establish credibility.

A good website puts a stake in the ground, telling your story and showing prospects:

- What your business is about

- The unique value you provide

- Which products and services you offer

- What makes you different

- Why your story is compelling

- How your brand makes a difference

- What it's like to work with (or for) your company

A website can also be used to capture leads, accept orders, provide updates or distribute information.

If you want your company to be taken seriously, you need a website to confirm that you're not a fly-by-night scam artist or an inexperienced hack. Like an entrepreneur who uses an old Hotmail or Yahoo account instead of a corporate email address, a business without a website is perceived as a hobby.

In fact, you should think of a website as your digital headquarters. Unlike social sites that can strip you of your credentials or remove your page at any time, often without warning or recourse, your company owns and controls its website.

Being in charge of the site lets you make updates at will, engage with visitors in the manner you choose, express the message you prefer, and build your brand as you see fit.

Even if you choose to have just a single page with contact information, a website serves as home base for your online presence. Treat it as you would a corporate office where you meet customers, partners, and prospective employees in person. Maintain your site and let it reflect the best possible view of your company.

What Makes a Website Good?

I had the honor of judging the Web Marketing Association's annual WebAwards competition for five years straight. One thing I observed during that time is how fast style changes in web design just as fashion changes in clothing, housewares and even automotive design.

It's fascinating to see how websites have evolved in a few short years. From Flash sites without much substance to sites that are so overloaded with keywords that they obscure the site's real purpose, much of web fashion is driven by technology.

One of the most dramatic changes has been the introduction of responsive design, enabling sites to dynamically render based on how they are accessed. A single site may appear differently on a desktop computer, laptop, tablet or cell phone.

This approach facilitates usability, making it easier for users to access the features most appropriate for their presumed intent, such as finding a store location on your mobile phone.

The approach may vary dramatically from industry to industry, but one thing is consistent among best-in-class websites. The designers and developers of those sites, as well as the executives directing their efforts, spent extensive time and effort understanding and catering to their users' needs.

If you want your website to represent you and your company well, keep the following in mind:

Design still matters. People like visually appealing websites. That's not to say that there aren't some very ugly sites that are highly effective, there are. (See the next bullet to learn why.) On the whole, your website design should be clean and simple, with graphics, images, and colors that complement your brand.

Visitors rule. Write your copy and design your site for users, not search engines. Who is going to use your site? Why are they coming? What do they want to accomplish? It only takes a fraction of a second for site visitors to vote "no" with a click of their mouse. If your bounce rate (the percentage of users that come to your site then leave right away) is high, then you're missing the mark.[16]

Usability trumps everything. The quality of a user's experience can mean the difference between a successful site and one that languishes with minimal traffic. Understand your audience and build a site that makes it easy for them to accomplish what they came for.

Are visitors placing online orders? Downloading an ebook or white paper? Scheduling a meeting? The right tools make these functions seamless. Test functions yourself and gather user feedback to improve your site.

Remember that not everyone has the same level of Internet savvy or physical ability. Many people are color blind, visually impaired, or simply unfamiliar with online tasks. Don't make life harder for these folks with light text on dark backgrounds (also called reverse text) or by using images with minimal contrast.

SEO is a tool, not a goal. From link building to keywords, if there is a technique that has been publicized as helpful for generating search traffic, someone has overdone it.

Avoid long lists of keywords, web copy that looks like a dissertation, and videos without descriptive text. These can all be turn-offs for users. If you make customers happy, they'll come back again and again and the search bots will follow.

With this information in mind, think back to that visit you took to your website at the start of this section. Do you see it in a different light, now? Does the message your site projects reflect the best face of your business? If not, it's time to get busy with some updates.

---

[16] What is considered high will depend on your industry and website history. As a rule of thumb, consider anything over 50% to be too high and work to encourage visitors to stay longer.

Don't Alienate Online Customers

If you followed all the preceding advice and your online presence still isn't meeting expectations, you might be inadvertently alienating online customers.

Watch for these issues:

1. **What exactly do you do?** It should be clear at first glance what business you're in. If you rely on stock photos and stale business jargon, customers will run away, fast. Clearly communicate what you do and why you're different, special, unique, or better than the rest.

2. **No phone number.** I know all the arguments for not listing a number. Your staff is busy. It costs money to provide phone support. Calls are a distraction. None of that matters. You *must* connect with customers. Add a phone number to your site.

3. **"Call for pricing."** Is your pricing so top secret that you can't show it online? If you need to work with prospects to develop custom quotes, say so. Otherwise, if you sell online, offer pricing online.

4. **Copyright date is two years ago.** Take a look at the footer on your page. Is the copyright notice current? An old date signals that your site is out of date. Why would a customer choose you over a competitor with a current site and fresh content?

5. **No return policy.** Or a "no return" policy. Making an online purchase is an act of faith. A missing return policy, or telling people, "Sorry, no returns," immediately raises questions. Stand behind what you sell and spell out your policies.

6. **Keyword overload.** If search engines can't tell what's most important about your site because you have too many keywords, it will rank poorly. Pick two or three words or phases for each page of your site. Write the copy for real people, and the search engines will follow.

7. **Lack of social proof.** Customers want proof that other people had a good experience with your business. Prove that you are not the

only one who thinks your business is awesome. Post legitimate testimonials, ratings and reviews, press clippings or articles that mention your business.

These ideas should give you a running start on making your site more customer-friendly. If you're guilty of any of these mistakes, fix them and see how your business improves.

Remember the Basics

These final tips may seem simple, but they are overlooked with surprising frequency. As you roll out your new site, be sure that you have done the following:

- If you redesigned an existing site, any pages that have been moved need to have "301 Redirects" set up so search engines will know where to find the new page. Your webmaster should be able to handle this for you.

- Create an XML sitemap and submit it to Google through their Webmaster Tools. This will tell Google what is on your site and what pages it should not index. (Note: This is *not* the same as the sitemap for users on your site. You need both.)

- Notify sites that link to your page of any updates needed to the URLs or website addresses they use. Update URLs for company profile pages across the web, and be sure your employees also update to the current website address on their profiles.

SEO: Where's Your Traffic?

"Help, I built a website and no one came!"

This is a common frustration when businesses invest thousands of dollars building fancy websites and the results are slow to materialize. Does it seem as if you've been waiting forever for business to roll in from your latest site redesign?

No matter how wonderful your new website is, traffic won't come just because you built it. Sure, the search bots at Google and Bing will find your site eventually, but you can't afford to twiddle your thumbs until then.

A website is just the beginning of a solid digital marketing effort. It can serve as the anchor for your campaigns, a place where visitors come to learn about your business and engage with your company.

The trick is, people have to find you first.

Getting your business discovered online is not hard, but it does take consistent effort to rank well for the targeted search terms that customers use to shop.

When you build a new website, there are a few things to consider from the start:

User-Friendly Copy. Your design and copy should be user-focused as well as search-friendly. Often, terms that rank well for SEO are not the ones you use to describe your products or services. Think like a customer and incorporate the keywords and phrases they use in your web copy.

Code matters. Your web developer should provide clean code that includes the proper meta tags (such as page titles and descriptions), correctly formatted images and links with anchor text.

Speed counts. A site should load quickly without bulky code and large images to slow things down. You can check how fast your site loads with Google's page speed utility, which will also provide tips on how to speed things up.[17]

Hopefully, you hired a web designer that understands SEO and these on-site factors are already incorporated into your new design. If not, make the fixes right away so you don't lose hard earned traffic as soon as it arrives.

If your site is small, say just 10-15 pages of content, it will be harder to rank highly in search results because you have less content to index. Regularly adding new content keeps your site fresh and encourages the search bots to stop by often, which can translate to higher rankings.

To expand your content, try posting customer reviews, video testimonials, photos of products, articles about your business, white papers or case studies, how-to information or FAQs. Make sure all of these materials include your carefully selected keywords.

Adding a blog gives you an opportunity to post fresh content regularly, inviting more people to visit and interact, which Google applauds. Videos are also a good magnet for traffic, if they are properly tagged and relevant to the content of your site.

(Not So) Secret SEO Solutions

You don't have to be an expert in search engine optimization to have a website that ranks well. Here are ten things to do to ensure your website is properly indexed by search engines.

If you're unsure how to implement these fixes, share the list with your web designer and ask them to do the work.

1. **Keywords in your URL**—if you are building a new site or changing your web page address, make sure your URL includes one of your top keywords. For example, if you own a pet grooming

---

[17] To check your page speed, visit
http://developers.google.com/speed/pagespeed/insights/

business, PetSpaGrooming.com is much more search-friendly than PetSpa.com.

2. **Every page is different**— whether you have five pages on your site or 500, search engines expect each page to be unique. Don't reuse the same page title or description on every page, and don't repeat the same content from page to page. Customize it.

3. **Use descriptive page titles**—These are specified in the <head> section of your page using the <title> tag, and should start with a keyword, not your company name. Search engines place more value on the first words in the title. *"Pet Grooming — Discriminating Dogs Choose PetSpa"* is more search-friendly than *"PetSpa — Dogs love being groomed here."*

4. **Keep titles short**—page titles should not be more than 65-70 characters, including spaces. The title not only helps with SEO, it also appears at the top of the web browser window, on the page tab and in the bookmark description, so it can make a big difference in site usability.

5. **Be mindful of description tags**—search engines often use the text in your page description, also set in the <head> section of the page, as the short snippet of copy displayed in search results. Use this as an opportunity to briefly describe what can be found on the page. Descriptions should be under 150 characters in length.

6. **Use images to your advantage**—correctly formatted images can help users find your site. Google and other search engines index images and display them in search results. When including an image on your site, use "alt" text to describe the image. Include relevant keywords. Rather than saying *"Drying Fido"* try *"Pet Drying Stations Complete the Grooming Process."*

7. **Optimize each page for just two or three keywords**—don't try to include every one of your keywords on each page of your site. Write your copy to highlight just two or three keywords that are appropriate for that page. Incorporate the selected keywords or phrases (called "long tail" search terms) into the text as naturally as possible.

8. **Keep web copy brief**—most web pages only need 250-300 words of copy. If your pages have much more than that, you should re-examine your content. You might be trying to cover too much information on a single page. Focus on your keywords, and keep your text short and to the point. This will help the search engines identify your key message and properly index your pages.

9. **Avoid large images**—search engines prefer text and hate to be bogged down loading large image files. Opening your website with a giant image pushes your text lower on the page. This tells the search engines that the content is not very important, and the page will not rank as highly. Compress image files and include important content above the fold (on the top half of the page).

10. **Use Headline Tags**—Using the html tags (<h1>, <h2>) to identify headlines tells search engines what is most important on your site. These tags can be easily styled using CSS (cascading style sheets) so they will be visually appealing as well as search friendly. Put your keywords in the headlines, and search engines will quickly find the most relevant content on the page.

Patience Pays

While it is tempting to expect instant results from your SEO efforts, patience and consistency are critical. It can take weeks or even months for changes on your website to have an impact on search rankings.

Don't give up too quickly. Monitor your site traffic with Google Analytics to see where visitors are coming from, what they like (the pages they spend the most time on), and what they don't. Pages with high bounce rates indicate visitors are leaving before they get through the door.

If you're having trouble and are not ranking as well as you think you should, use Google Webmaster Tools to identify issues with broken links, missing pages or slow page load times.

Keep adding relevant content, posting, linking, and sharing, and your hard work will eventually pay off.

Extend Your Reach with Digital Media

On-site SEO is only half the equation for getting found online. What you do to proactively drive traffic to your site is the other half. Cast a wider net by moving beyond your website to other channels, such as blogs and social media to generate inbound links and build interest in your site. More ways to generate traffic include:

- Offer interesting articles and downloadable content.

- Add your website address to all your online profiles.

- Encourage employees to link to your company site from their social media profiles on places like LinkedIn.

- Include your website address when you comment on blogs or post on forums related to your business.

- Try advertising with Google AdWords or other online ad partners like Bing, Yahoo or Facebook.

- Include your website URL in offline advertising.

Also, be sure your company listings are accurate on sites like Manta, Jigsaw, and other digital directories. Don't forget industry associations and their online member directories for business profiles that link to your site.

Wherever your company is listed, complete the profiles and add your website so that your company can be easily found.

Paid, Earned and Owned

You may have heard people talk about "paid, earned and owned" media and wondered what, exactly, that means. In the world of digital marketing strategy, different media types play distinctive roles.

The following table illustrates the basic differences between each of these:

Table 7

Type	What It Is	How It's Used
Paid	Purchased impressions, such as pay-per-click ads, display ads and sponsorships.	To create traffic for your owned media, generate leads, promote sales or offers.
Owned	Your digital properties, including websites, blogs, and social media accounts.	Capture leads, share valuable content, establish thought leadership, educate customers, and convert sales.
Earned	Visibility achieved through word of mouth, publicity, social shares and online buzz.	Build trust and credibility, increase interest and awareness, and generate low-cost, high-value traffic and leads.

We've already covered your website, and the tips I shared apply to your other owned media, like blogs, as well. Now, let's explore paid and earned media.

PPC and digital advertising

There are lots of ways to run ads online, from text-based ads using keywords to banner ads on sponsored sites. Google AdWords and Facebook ads are both popular and affordable solutions to generate traffic and secure leads.

If you want to quickly build an email list or drive traffic to a new website or blog, well-placed online advertising can be very effective.

This is an area where a DIY approach can be successful. However, it takes a lot of work and knowledge to actively manage campaigns and monitor results. Frequent adjustments are required to keep up with ever-changing traffic patterns. Trends, news cycles and even seasonality can affect your ROI.

Rather than trying to keep up with all of this yourself, I recommend getting a professional partner to help. Stay in touch regularly and carefully monitor your spending.

For starters, watch these key metrics:

- **Cost-per-click:** How much do you pay for each click on an ad? It might be pennies or several dollars; either is OK *if* you get good value. Set a baseline and monitor trends for changes that may signal a problem.

- **Conversion rates:** How many sales does your campaign generate? Does one in every three visitors buy, for example?

- **Traffic generated:** How much traffic can you attribute to your PPC and display ads? Is it good quality traffic (translating into lots of buyers) or poor?

- **Bounce rate:** How much paid traffic leaves your site right after it arrives? If the percentage is high, try improving alignment between your ads and landing pages.

Surprisingly, strong results from paid advertising can also improve your search rankings. Why? Because the search engines like to see visitors spend time on a site and complete transactions.

When many people "vote" for your site with behavior that signals they like what they find, your site will rank higher than others that don't yield good results.

Earned media

Traffic due to publicity and social shares is highly valuable. Although it's free in the sense that you don't pay for it directly, many online marketers invest significantly in building earned media impressions.

Viral videos, sponsored social campaigns and content marketing are all paid efforts to attract attention that leads to earned media. If you do these things well, they can take off through social sharing or others blogging about your business.

A home run in earned media is the equivalent of being quoted by the Wall Street Journal or New York Times. Having a celebrity blogger or a social media rock star mention your business can ignite a wildfire of coverage.

When this happens, be ready to engage with site visitors. Respond to comments quickly, answer any questions that arise, and enjoy riding the wave. Make sure you capture leads along the way so you can follow-up on these budding relationships once the buzz dies down.

Find the Right Mix

Believe it or not, there's more to marketing than digital. Balancing online and offline techniques will usually lead to better results than placing all your focus on one or the other.

To create an effective, integrated marketing plan, first determine your goals. Draw a line from these goals to your customers. How do they connect?

- Are you launching a new product?
- Breaking into a new market?
- Trying to increase sales of existing products?

Each of these objectives requires a different approach.

Some tools are better than others for things like immediate response, lead generation, and awareness. For example, a print campaign in a trade publication can be a good way to build brand awareness over time, but it's unlikely to generate immediate sales.

Online marketing can support lead generation goals with content marketing that effectively positions your company as a leader in the industry. Things like PPC or social campaigns can convert sales and create brand advocacy.

Some key questions to consider when deciding on your media mix:

Where are your customers? If they don't use Facebook or Twitter, you don't really need a presence there. Social media can be enticing, but it takes a lot of time and effort to do it right. Be sure you're committed before jumping into social programs.

Likewise, if you're going to advertise online, find the right sites to place your ads. Think beyond PPC to display ads, content marketing and promotions on sites your customers visit regularly. Consider mobile, apps and other vehicles as well.

How can you get the best impact from your investments? The number of people you reach is not as important as reaching the right people. If fact, dealing with too many unqualified leads can create problems if your business has limited resources.

Look for opportunities to connect with highly targeted groups that are receptive to your marketing messages. This might be done through direct mail or other offline programs (seminars, events, etc.) rather than online campaigns.

Can digital enhance your traditional marketing? If you already have strong traditional marketing programs such as a print newsletter, think about using digital to improve the ROI. Repurposing content is an excellent way to get more for your money.

Print articles can be redistributed as blog posts or shared as content on your website, for example. Moving some of your traditional campaigns online might also reduce your overall marketing costs, improving your net return.

Social Media Smarts

Over the past several years, social media has evolved from a novelty to a practical business tool with the ability to deliver real results.

If you've been waiting on the sidelines and are finally ready to get your feet wet, read this section. If you're a social media veteran, skip ahead to learn how to improve your social media ROI (page 188).

Getting Started with Social Media

Stake out your territory

If you haven't already claimed your spot on social media, do it now. Establishing a consistent social media presence is just as important as protecting your trademarks and other intellectual property. Look beyond the "Big Three" (Twitter, Facebook, and LinkedIn) to protect your brand. Create corporate profiles on a variety of social media sites, even if you don't intend to use them right away.

Tools like knowem.com will search availability on over 500 sites and help you claim your company name on social networks across the web.

Put your ear to the ground

Listen to what's being said about your company and competitors. Use tools like Google Alerts or more sophisticated enterprise solutions to monitor terms like your company and product names as well as those of competitors and industry thought leaders.

Having a social listening program in place is vital. Assign the listening task to Customer Service or Marketing so team members can respond—in real time—to comments or conversations online. Proactively addressing both positive and negative feedback will win you a loyal following.

Find your corporate voice

When employees are tweeting, blogging, and sharing on social media as representatives of your company, it's important that they embody your corporate voice.

They don't need to work from a prescribed script and should not sound like robots. Instead, let your employees' personalities shine through while expressing corporate values, brand personality, and your philosophy for doing business.

This requires extra training to ensure employees understand and believe in your brand. They must internalize your brand values in order to share them in a natural way.

Use cross-functional social media messaging workshops to give staff an opportunity to practice conversational tweets and posts that are on-message without sounding stiff or stilted.

Add value

Social media is about sharing more than selling. Consistently adding value creates goodwill that will eventually lead to sales. Share information that customers need, even if it is not directly related to your product or service.

Create community among your followers and encourage them to engage each other as well as your company. If you have a social listening program in place, you'll be able to hear what people are saying online and add your thoughts when appropriate.

You can promote your company occasionally; just don't overdo it. Customers appreciate periodic special offers, discounts, or "members only" insights, provided these are not the sole focus of your social media efforts.

Set the guidelines

Last on my list, but most important of all: If you have more than one employee, your company needs guidelines for social media use. Unlike a restrictive Internet Usage Policy that outlines everything employees can't do, your social media policy should empower employees.

Address not only how they will engage with customers and prospects from company accounts, but also how they talk about your business on their own.

Think in terms of what you want employees to do to support your brand, from proactive outreach to joining existing conversations. Give them space with reasonable boundaries and employees can be a powerful force for building your brand online. (*Learn more in* Create a Social Media Policy *on page 195.*)

Find the ROI in Social Media

Earning a return on your investments in social media is critical, but not easy. Duke University's annual CMO survey has persistently shown that less than 7% of respondents view social media as "very integrated" to their firm's strategy. In 2014, nearly 14.8% rated social media as "not at all integrated."[18]

Even in the world of social media, results matter. If you're struggling to see the bottom line impact of social media, it's time to take a broader view. Think beyond social media as a stand-alone function or nice-to-have tool and get strategic about your approach.

Is social worth the time?

As social media becomes an essential component of almost any marketing plan, every company needs to keep an eye on the ROTI (return on time invested).

In spite of popular perceptions, social media isn't really free. While you can set up accounts on social media platforms like Twitter, Facebook, LinkedIn and Google+ without spending a dime out of pocket, the price of tools to manage these accounts ranges from free to hundreds, even thousands of dollars a month.

Potentially even more expensive is the time required to post, monitor, report and evaluate social media initiatives. You must be attuned to the ROTI of your employees' social media efforts, especially if social media is only one aspect of their job.

Can your company afford for busy employees to spend hours a day building a following on Twitter, pinning on Pinterest, and connecting on Google+?

There is a real opportunity cost to social media. What are you or your employees *not* doing while working on social networking? If you are just playing around without clear objectives, you're probably missing out on other more important opportunities.

To avoid this, gather your team and have a frank discussion about why you are engaging in social media. Then map out your objectives and develop a focused social media plan:

---

[18] Christine Moorman. 2014. *CMO Survey Report: Highlights and Insights, Feb. 2014.* https://faculty.fuqua.duke.edu/cmosurveyresults/The_CMO_Survey-Highlights_and_Insights-Feb-2014.pdf (accessed March 14, 2014).

- Do you want to engage with potential customers?

- Are you hoping to catch the attention of the media?

- Would you like to recruit new employees?

- Do you hope to attract prospective business partners?

Figure out which of these are priorities, and how you will reach the right people. Anything else is just noise.

Once you know who to reach, figure out where those people hang out. You don't need to be on all the major social media networks if your targeted contacts spend most of their time on just one or two platforms. A little knowledge about buyers' social media habits will greatly increase your ROTI by reducing wasted effort.

Get focused in your messaging and be intentional about what you share. Don't kill time tweeting about topics that aren't relevant to your audience, or sharing content that doesn't add value to the relationships you are building. Laser focus is essential to high social media ROTI.

Should CEOs Use Social Media?

It depends. If you can truly be the voice of your company, go ahead. Share an occasional comment, announcement, or point of interest. Keep in mind that what you say, and how you say it, will be watched carefully.

If you are not comfortable creating an executive presence online, it's better not to go there in the first place. Don't delegate your personal account to an employee or agency. There is no way someone else can represent your unique view from the top. Do it yourself or don't do it at all.

Setting Your Social Strategy

Effective use of social media has evolved well beyond simply setting up accounts on Twitter and Facebook. Social media has become a strategic imperative for companies that reaches beyond the walls of the marketing department to touch every facet of the organization.

Social maturity is an intentional approach to social media as part of a holistic marketing and business strategy. It's no longer a "shiny object" with the simple aim of electing fans and followers. Today, the goal of social media is to create advocates and build brand equity.

This requires a social strategy designed to support corporate objectives. Social engagement should reach all corners of your company, enabling employees to connect with customers, partners, prospective employees and even each other.

Figure 12: Social Strategy Evolution

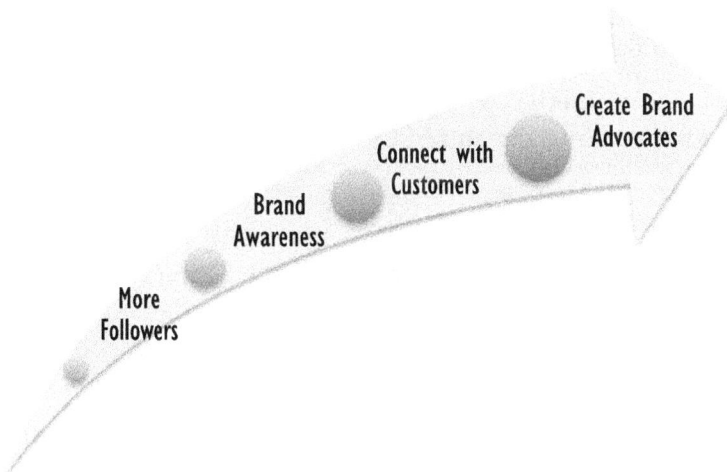

As you implement social media, there are several ways to ensure your organization's success:

- **Embrace Operational Integration:** An attitude of "It's how we do business," means making social an integral part of the way you do business (not just another activity).

- **Build Cross Functional Teams:** Create teams to take social beyond the marketing domain. Include representatives from sales, customer service, PR, product and other areas.

- **Create Centers of Excellence:** If you have a larger company, establish of social "centers of excellence" or resource centers to provide internal support and best practices.

- **Choose Metrics that Matter:** Define and align social media metrics and measurements with business strategies and your other marketing tactics.

Social Media is a Spice for Marketing

Think of social media as the seasoning to spice up your marketing. It can easily be added to your existing marketing efforts, helping you connect with customers and build relationships.

Integrate social media with complementary marketing tactics like email, content marketing and SEO.

Email marketing goes social

There's more to integrating email and social than simply adding an icon. Social media campaigns can be distributed via social channels like Twitter, and requests to share and promote can be included in web-based emails.

Failure to include a social call-to-action in a marketing email is a tremendous oversight. It should be standard procedure for email campaign development.

Use your emails to reward followers, connecting members of your social network with special incentives and recognition:

- Segment email lists by social platform (i.e. Facebook fans).

- Target distinct social groups with special promotions.

- Promote exclusive offers or rewards to active connections.

- Offer incentives to connect on multiple platforms.

Look beyond typical marketing messages to take advantage of email communications across the organization. You can add social integration in a number of ways:

1. Include personal or corporate social media accounts on employee email signatures.

2. Add invitations to connect via social media to welcome messages and thank you emails.

3. Include social media links on customer service messages, such as post-chat transcripts or survey requests.

4. Include social sharing options on survey invitations to increase response rates.

5. Segment email lists to target selected social groups (such as Facebook fans) with special promotions.

Social spreads content

Content marketing is all about being magnetic. Using blogs, articles, white papers, and other materials to generate website traffic is the goal, and social makes it happen.

Developing content can be expensive if outsourced and time consuming when done in-house. Fortunately, once it's complete, it can be repurposed across the web.

Integrate keywords into these materials to drive traffic to content that is subsequently shared through social channels.

Popular types of content that users enjoy and promote include:

- Videos
- Newsletter articles
- Blogs
- White papers
- Twitter #hashtag series[19]

---

[19] This is a series of Tweets identified by a common hashtag that is unique to your message, like #WhenToSendFlowers.

Social improves SEO

More than half (55%) of respondents in a 2012 survey by Social Media Examiner indicated improvements in search rankings as a result of using social media.[20]

As proof of the strong connection between social and search, Google introduced Social Search to personalize search results back in 2009 and Bing incorporated Facebook results in 2010.

Today, Google gives added weight to sites with lots of social activity, pushing rankings for popular content higher, especially when tied to Google+.

The term Social Media Optimization (SMO) reflects the incorporation of search engine optimization tactics into social media.

The most basic way to leverage SEO in social is to utilize keyword research. From seeding keywords into your marketing content to planting them in your posts, carefully selected keywords can successfully drive qualified traffic to your website.

Invest the time to understand trending topics that are relevant to your industry and develop a keyword list for your social media communications. Don't forget to incorporate appropriate keywords into hashtags on Twitter, company profiles, blogs, video tags and other social posts.

You can also use SEO and keywords to drive traffic to your content that is subsequently shared through social channels. Be sure that any content you publish has links to your social networks and calls-to-action to invite sharing.

Keywords change over time, and what you, as an industry expert, search for may not be the same as the words and phrases that customers use. Regular research and ongoing monitoring are essential to keep your keyword list relevant.

---

[20] Stelzner, Michael A. 2012. *2012 Social Media Marketing Industry Report: How Marketers Are Using Social Media to Grow Their Businesses.* Social Media Examiner. http://www.socialmediaexaminer.com/social-media-marketing-industry-report-2012/

Measuring Social Success

Your specific goals and objectives for social media should flow from your strategy, and align with the overall vision and mission of your business.

Rather than emphasizing arbitrary numbers like how many friends or followers you have, your goals should focus on more meaningful items such as:

Engagement—How much interaction happens between your company and its followers? Do people comment on your blog posts, share your articles on LinkedIn, and respond to your questions on Twitter?

Reach—Look beyond your immediate audience to your audience's networks. If you have influential followers, you'll gain more visibility when they comment and share your content with their audience. This is a ripple effect, like a pebble in a pond.

Conversions—How do your online connections translate into measurable business opportunities? Does social media generate leads, website visits, product subscriptions, or downloads? Define conversion on your own terms, as long as the focus is on taking action towards a sale.

Sentiment—A reflection of your online reputation, sentiment will tell you if the buzz about your business is positive, neutral, or negative. It doesn't all need to be rosy, but neutral to favorable should be the baseline.

Once you have established realistic goals, work with your team to create a social strategy and tactical plan that will achieve them.

Create a Social Media Policy

If you haven't established a social media policy for your business, it's time to get one.

Like an Internet Use policy, a social media policy explains how employees can utilize social media when representing the company. If it hasn't been updated lately, your Internet Use policy probably doesn't cover social media. Protect yourself, your brand, and your employees with a well-written set of guidelines to govern social media use.

You can buy templates online or get a sample from your social media consultant to get started.[21] You'll want to tailor these guidelines to the unique aspects of your business, incorporating any generally accepted practices for your industry.

As with any legal document, it's smart to seek legal advice when developing a social media policy for your business. Your attorney can advise you on local laws, privacy concerns, and other issues to consider when defining the terms of your policy.

In drafting your guidelines, let employees know what they can do in addition to what is prohibited. The idea is not to be rigid and restrictive. Good guidelines allow employees to engage confidently in social media because they understand what is expected and encouraged, not just what to avoid.

Some important items to address in your policy include:

Disclosures and Transparency—Insist that employees are open and transparent about whether they are posting on behalf of the company or not. Personal opinions about products and other issues related to the company need to be identified as such.

Privacy and Security—Include instructions on how to protect personal privacy and corporate information on social networks. Provide specific details about what privacy settings should be used for company accounts.

Honesty and Ethics—Incorporate your corporate code of ethics into your social media policy. Highlight any specific concerns about honesty in online postings, from information on individual profiles to status updates and blog postings.

---

[21] You can download a sample Social Media Policy Template for free at http://howbizgrows.com/free-marketing-resources/social-media-policy-template/

Confidential and Proprietary Information—Remind employees of their obligation to protect confidential information belonging to the company, its vendors, and customers.

Personal and Corporate Profiles—What does your company consider appropriate (or inappropriate) on a social media profile? Address expectations regarding profile pictures, bios, and company descriptions. Clearly point out what would be considered unacceptable.

Use of Images, Copyrighted and Trademarked Materials—How will you protect your brand online? Let employees know what the correct format is for copyright and trademark attribution. Include guidelines on selection of images and requirements for photo credits, model releases, and use of images found online or produced by others.

Respect and Consideration—Courtesy online is important. When employees get caught up in a heated discussion on social networks, unraveling the PR mess that may follow can be an expensive proposition. State your policies regarding posting emotional remarks and disparaging, offensive, or discriminatory comments. Address potential problems before they happen, and let employees know what recourse will be taken for violations.

Ownership of Corporate Social Media Accounts—Are your company's social media accounts tied to personal email addresses? If so, when employees leave, access to those accounts goes with them. Use your policy to clarify what happens when an employee separates from the company, including who owns the account and how access will be transferred to another staffer.

Social media policies need to be updated regularly to minimize risk. Revisit your policy at least once a year to ensure new platforms and technologies are addressed.

Chapter 10

What's Next?

By now you should have a running start on accelerated business growth. Have you been applying what you learned here as you move from chapter to chapter? If so, you are probably seeing results already, and I hope that progress has inspired you to do more.

If you powered through this entire book without stopping to implement any changes, then I encourage you to go back and revisit a few selected sections.

Find the areas that hold the most promise for your business in terms of added value. Tackle a few of the items in the chapter on that topic, and see what happens. By dedicating your efforts in a focused way, you'll see results more quickly than if you attempt to do too much at once.

As you work through the exercises and advice I've provided here, you may realize that you need additional support or simply want to continue learning. If that's the case, visit my business growth website, HowBizGrows.com for some free resources.

You'll discover an ever-expanding community of business owners to share your experiences with, along with timesaving tools and templates you can download for free.

My blog at JoeySargent.com is another invaluable source of information and fresh approaches to business growth. I provide practical advice and content that motivates and sustains readers though this exciting journey. As a preview, I adapted a few of those posts to share with you here.

Captive in the Comfort Zone

In my work as a business growth strategist, I talk with people every day who want desperately to move forward. They have high standards for themselves, and big dreams for their companies. They also have a nagging feeling that *something isn't right*.

Many would-be achievers share a common challenge: they're having trouble creating the escape velocity needed to break free of their own gravity.

Which Way to Success?

I've observed three distinct ways entrepreneurs navigate their path to success. With persistence, they can all yield results, but one route stands out as more efficient than others:

Follow the path of least resistance

This approach results in a long and winding road. Meandering from point to point based on the ease of the path ahead makes it possible to avoid conflict and discord. Unfortunately, it's not an expeditious way to get where you're going.

People who follow this path are often unsure where they really want to go. Instead, they seize upon any opportunity that crosses their path. Customers and employees often become frustrated with the lack of direction. As a result, they leave for competitors that have a clear vision, slowing progress even more.

Creep along in the comfort zone

Leaders who stay between the lines can get ahead, but they tend to take three steps forward and two steps back. This pattern of acceleration is one in which they spring forward when inspiration strikes, and then fall back when resistance appears.

Why the constant backtracking? It's a byproduct of the assumption that when something new doesn't work, it is easier to retreat and go with what you know.

Sticking close to the comfort zone is a more tentative than purposeful approach. It's indicative of a leader who fears the potential for failure, and as result, misses key opportunities to accelerate business growth.

Take the direct route

We all learned in school that the shortest distance between two points is a straight line, but that doesn't make the direct approach an easy one. Going full throttle requires the fortitude to push hard against barriers, enjoying the rush of momentum that follows a breakthrough.

Often executives who employ this route find internal and external resistance. People who prefer the path of least resistance tell them it's not worth the fight. Those who feel safest in the comfort zone beg them to slow down and "think about it."

Instead, these leaders forge ahead. They know what they want, and they go for it.

If you're struggling to reach your goals, investing a little time to think about your approach can be revealing:

- Do you envision your style as direct, but fall back into the comfort zone whenever things get rocky?

- Are you full of great ideas, but afraid to execute then?

- Do you convince yourself that "it's just too hard" to meet competitors head on?

If any of the above is true, you could be a willing captive in your own prison. *Find the key and break free.*

Get a Fresh Perspective

If you seem to be stuck on some particularly troublesome business issues, this little fable about my friend Ann, her husband Sam and their friend Chuck may hold the solution. *(Names have been changed to protect the guilty.)*

One day Ann and Sam decided that it was time to replace the garage door opener. After finding a great online bargain for a high quality opener, they decided to save a little money and have Sam install it himself.

Sam, being a little less than super-handy thought, "I should get my friend Chuck to help." Chuck is one of those guys that everyone needs as a friend or neighbor. He has a truck full tools and the know-how to use them. Best of all, he can usually be paid with beer.

The next afternoon, Sam and Chuck got together and started working on the door opener. They took down the old one, opened the new one, and quickly assembled it. In almost no time they were ready to tackle installation.

Then before they knew it, Chuck and Sam were in trouble. Their speedy project plan came to a screeching halt when the opener wouldn't fit properly.

After a couple of hours of scratching their heads, re-reading the instructions, and measuring over and over, they thought they found the problem.

"It's missing two holes," they decided.

What to do? A simple solution was evident: drill two new holes.

Soon Ann arrived home and they explained their predicament. "There was something wrong with this opener," they said. "It was missing two holes. But we made new ones and we're ready to put it up."

An hour later dinnertime was approaching and Ann stepped outside to see how things were going. Chuck and Sam were puzzled, "It still won't open right," Sam said. "We can't figure out what's wrong. It should work, but it doesn't," explained Chuck.

Eventually, Chuck and Sam decided to call it a day. After a well-deserved beer, Chuck went home and Sam felt defeated.

The opener was up. It opened the garage door...most of the way. It just wasn't working quite right.

The next morning Sam went off to work, cursing the faulty opener and vowing to get it fixed over the weekend.

Ann was frustrated too, so she decided to check things out herself.

She grabbed a ladder, climbed up and took a good look. Ann could see the adjustment the men had made, but she refused to believe that the opener made it through manufacturing and inspection without two critical holes.

After consulting the instructions, Ann turned to YouTube to see what she could find. In about five minutes, she was watching a video that showed, in detail, how to properly install the opener.

Ann toted her iPad up the ladder, reviewed the video again, and noticed something the men didn't see. The opener itself was installed **backwards!**

How could two smart men have missed that?

Actually, it was an easy mistake.

Working together, Chuck and Sam developed a shared point of view. Their mutual trust and common perspective affirmed to each of them that the path they chose was correct. Once decided, they were committed to their course of action and didn't (or couldn't) step back far enough to see what was really going on.

It was only with a fresh perspective and the aid of some additional input that the problem was solved.

Beyond Home Improvement

Homeowners aren't the only ones who fall prey to misplaced assumptions. Scenarios like this play out in businesses every day.

A group of smart people gets together. They firmly believe that their shared knowledge and experience is all they need to solve the problems they face.

Unfortunately, they may not even be looking at the right problem. Like Chuck and Sam, who were convinced the door opener was faulty, the team's assumptions get in the way. They agree on what's wrong. They think they know how to fix it.

But making holes, or plugging them, isn't the right solution when the problem is one of orientation:

- Hiring top talent won't solve a problem with excess employee attrition.

- Sales performance isn't your problem if they're selling the wrong products.

- Competition might not be to blame for customer defections if you have surly employees running them off.

Finding the right solution is only possible when you have the proper perspective.

If you're stuck on a thorny issue, or one that keeps popping up every time you think you've got it solved, it's time for you to get a fresh take on the situation.

Step back in order to break out of tunnel vision or team myopia. Get someone else to look at the problem so you can truly see it clearly. Turn to a trusted advisor, bring in a consultant, or engage a different group of employees to take a look at the circumstances.

You'll be surprised by how many of the "immovable" roadblocks in your organization suddenly become less stubborn.

Why the "Safe Choice" Should Scare You

How often have you been faced with a difficult decision and decided to go with the safe bet instead of taking a gamble?

Conventional wisdom holds that avoiding risk is the best thing for business leaders. We hear about minimizing risk, risk mitigation, and many other expressions that reinforce the idea that we should play it safe.

But should you?

Sometimes the safe choice isn't nearly as secure as it should be.

- Seeking safety in the *status quo* ensures that those who aren't afraid to proceed will leave you behind.

- Seeking safety in the comfort zone means you'll keep doing what seems to work. Until it doesn't.

- Seeking safety in tradition can leave you hanging on to outmoded ideas while someone else is thinking bigger.

Let me challenge you to the think about the safe choices you make every day in a different way. What if safety is exactly what you should *avoid*? Skip the reckless decisions, but try calculated risks.

It's like the difference between jumping off a bridge and bungee jumping. Both will give you a thrill, but only one ends well.

Safety isn't failsafe. Opting for the safe choice is usually a decision made from a position of fear, not strength.

When leaders worry that change will hurt, they take the safe route. Executives who don't want to let go cling to safe choices. Employees who fear retribution make safe decisions that result in missed opportunities. Buyers choose the safe option to reduce perceived risk, while unwittingly sacrificing the rewards of something new.

Think about this...

- Safety is the enemy of innovation.

- Safety is the enemy of progress.

- Safety is the enemy of growth.

So, do you really want to play it safe?

It's Your Time to Soar

You took a big risk starting your business. You made bold choices to get where you are today. Now you're beyond the launch and it's time to soar.

I hope you've enjoyed this book, and that it has helped you see the potential in your future. Forget the odds and ignore the doomsayers who remind you how many businesses fail. You've got the tools you need to create a business that thrives. Apply them diligently and I'm sure you will succeed.

Index

Acknowledgements

This book would not have become a reality without incredible support from a number of wonderful people. I'd especially like to thank the following friends and colleagues who have been steadfast in their encouragement and advice:

To my friend and colleague, Kimberly Collins, for monthly coffee marathons and holding me accountable when my resolve wavered.

Brandy Nagle, Jenny Munn and Anita Hample, thanks for the laughs when I needed them and no-holds-barred feedback over breakfast.

Much appreciation to Beverly Helton for your patience in sharing my ups and downs and for being a great listener, and to Wynell Lauver for your prowess in proofreading.

Many thanks to Jeff Sheehan, one of my original "Twitter friends," for being there IRL (in real life) as an advocate and sounding board.

Farmer John and Writer Kate, thanks for not throwing me overboard when you had the chance! I love you.

Finally, to Jim, Alyssa and Erin, I'm so lucky you love me! Thanks for standing by while I've been consumed by this project and for believing in me, no matter what. You're everything to me.

About the Author

Joellyn 'Joey' Sargent decided to forge her own path in 2010, after 22 years as a corporate marketing executive. Her award-winning career includes roles with Fortune 500 organizations like UPS and BellSouth (now AT&T), early-stage start-ups and her own small businesses.

Today, Joey works with business owners and senior leaders, creating powerful momentum for business growth. As founder and president of the Claravon Consulting Group, she provides the clarity, vision and insight that leaders need to achieve their goals.

Joey connects strategic thinking with execution at the point of maximum impact, creating compelling customer experiences. As a result, her clients consistently deliver breakthrough results in performance, revenue, and profitability.

Through her writing, speaking and consulting, Joey offers fresh perspectives and no-nonsense advice on how to grow a business while staying true to personal priorities. She is frequently quoted in the media on strategy, leadership and branding.

Joey attended Duke University and graduated from Eckerd College in St. Petersburg, FL where she discovered a love for international travel. She earned an MBA from Embry-Riddle Aeronautical University.

Joey can be reached through Claravon Consulting at 678.823.8228 or online at Claravon.com.

Joey's blogs: JoeySargent.com I HowBizGrows.com
Twitter: @JoellynSargent

Additional Resources

eBooks by Joellyn Sargent on Amazon.com:

Meet Your Ideal Customer

Is That You…Or Your Brand?

The *Powerful Customer Relationships* series:

> You Can't Please Everyone—Finding the Right Customers for Exponential Growth
>
> Inside-Out: How Corporate Culture Impacts Customer Experience
>
> Beyond Delight: How to Build Customer Relationships that Last

Business Momentum Index – Use this quick assessment to determine how your business is doing. Download the free tool at: www.Claravon.com/resources/ business-momentum-index

Join Joey's Community at HowBizGrows.com to access resources like these:

- Sales Toolkit Checklist
- Communications Plan Template
- Event Promotions Planning Calendar

Thrive! Get the free monthly newsletter at Claravon.com

www.ingramcontent.com/pod-product-compliance
Lightning Source LLC
Chambersburg PA
CBHW060548200326
41521CB00007B/528